The Pink & Purple Sky

My story of being caregiver wife to my cancer-fighting Warrior husband, juggling motherhood to our 5 kids and a love that never left.

NUR EZMIEN MOHD YATIM

To order additional copies of this book, contact
Toll Free +65 3165 7531 (Singapore)
Toll Free +60 3 3099 4412 (Malaysia)
www.partridgepublishing.com/singapore
orders.singapore@partridgepublishing.com

Because of the dynamic nature of the Internet, any web addresses or links contained in this book may have changed since publication and may no longer be valid. The views expressed in this work are solely those of the author and do not necessarily reflect the views of the publisher, and the publisher hereby disclaims any responsibility for them.

ISBN
ISBN: 978-1-5437-7133-6 (sc)
ISBN: 978-1-5437-7134-3 (hc)
ISBN: 978-1-5437-7132-9 (e)

Print information available on the last page.

09/16/2022

PARTRIDGE

CONTENTS

Al Fatihah for my Warrior,

Kekanda Selamat bin Kassim.

Love is forever and a day, always.

Never ending love for our children,

Arfan Firas, Sarah Nur Ezzati, Eshan Firdaus,

Naela Nur Hanis, and Nadra Nur Aysha,

The Selamat Entourage.

ONE
12 July 2022/12 Zulhijjah 1443

I guessed I should be ready for this. Afterall, the doctor had said he wouldn't last past a year. I have seen his body deteriorating.

At 7:40 a.m. that day, I lost my husband. My Warrior. My companion.

No amount of preparation could have softened the blow as I stood by his bedside and asked, "Are you there, Abang?"

Only to be staring at a lifeless body, staring back at me. Towards the end of his days, my warrior was unable to close his right eye. Cancer had slowly ravaged his body over three years and affected much of his facial ability over the last weeks, more on his right side. I had noticed that his left eye was also refusing to shut as frequently a few days back. So there I was looking at him as if he was looking back at me.

I took out the oxygen concentrator tube from his nose gently and hugged him. I said my last apologies as I lay my head on his chest. That chest was all bony, but it used to be my thick source of comfort. He was always generous with his hugs for me. Every time I needed it, he'll pull me close. Even when I'm angry at him, he'll pull me close, and instantly, the anger subsided. My Warrior's chest was where I loved to lie on and felt completely safe.

I kissed his lips, forehead several times, cheeks, chin, and chest. I said "thank you." I said "I love you." I said "I will miss you." I ran my hands on his thin arms. The arms that held me close. The arms that I slept on. The arms that carried our babies. I held his feet, where my *Syurga* is. My paradise. I had massaged those

1

tired feet dutifully. I placed my hand beneath his as though to have him hold my hand for the last time. This was the hand that would always find mine, held on walks, crossing the road, when I'm nervous or anxious, when I want to fall asleep, and anytime in between when there was nothing else the hands were busy with. These hands would hold mine tightly and wouldn't let me go when I'm angry.

"Hold hands 'til we wrinkle," he had said. His handsome, dimpled smile and kind eyes would greet me.

I took a long look at his face. He was the guy I had fallen so madly in love with. I could never be mad for too long at that face. The face that lit up every time I entered the room. I got butterflies every time he walked into to the room. My handsome one.

I said my personal farewell. I kissed his right hand for the last time.

This was what you wanted, Kekanda. Last breath in our house.

Calls ensued soon after as I did what I had to, informing the key people that my Warrior has left; to the children's schools, informing them that the children will need to be home. It's few more minutes of just my Warrior and me before the house was filled with people. Before I am all alone facing the world. His *kain ihram* from our recent and only *Umrah* together covered his body.

Everything that happened that day, forever etched in my heart.

TWO

#mrselamatsilatsthecancer #papaof5fightscancer

July 2019. It was a scene that you watched on many medical dramas.

"I'm sorry to have to break this to you. Mr Selamat, it is cancer."

Just a week after the initial scan, the doctor at the ENT Centre at Singapore General Hospital sadly broke the news. I went blank for like three minutes. Just how does one react to this? What does a wife typically do? What does a mother of five generally do? Do I start bawling now? Do I start thinking of the worst? Do I start researching all sorts of remedy? Do I ask the doctor to check his notes again? How should I be feeling? At first, I thought, where did I go wrong in the simplest job of taking care of my husband? Why didn't I ask him to get that little lump on his neck checked before it grew? Wives carry with us such responsibility that it is just unthinkable how things could go wrong. On that day, he began his life as our cancer Warrior. And I became a caregiver.

In 2013, my Warrior had a major L4L5 spinal operation. In 2015, he had an emergency operation to remove his timebomb of an appendix. In 2019, he was diagnosed with nasopharyngeal cancer. Is just leading a normal, non-eventful life too easy for him? All these medical speedbumps, is it necessary? However, I believe no one is tested beyond our capabilities. God sets challenges for us because he knows we can handle it. Trust and keep the faith.

A week after that, the process began. Starting with a trip to the National Dental Centre. Prior to treatments, oral health needs to be checked. A couple of loose teeth were taken out. It was anticipated that with radiation treatment, a few more oral issues may pop up.

Then it was measurements taken for the shell for radiation, PET scan, MRI, and CT simulation. Everything was done on express. The Warrior was a Stage 4B by the time he was diagnosed. Survival rate: 60%. They needed to get him on treatment as soon as possible. The days that followed were appointments after appointments.

Every day 35 people in Singapore are diagnosed with cancer. A scary reality that I read on a sticker on a lift panel at the National Cancer Centre, my second office for the coming weeks. I had told my employer of what was going on, and they immediately understood the situation and offered support. I could work off-site on treatment and appointment days. And if I ever needed to urgently take the time off work, they gave the go-ahead. They were incredibly supportive and sensitive. For which I am thankful for.

However, sensitivity was not always the thing with some.

"What stage?" One of the first questions people asked when we announced that my Warrior has cancer. I didn't realise how sensitive this question is until we were faced with it. Here's the thing: You do not get "staged" the moment you're diagnosed. I blamed movies and TV dramas for this. But this is not TV. They break the news that you have cancer, and then you need a couple of scans before you can get "staged." It became a stressful question, at least to me, because I didn't really want to hear the stage thing. It made no difference because treatment still needs to be planned, and there was a huge turn in our lives which I had no idea how I was going to handle. And truthfully, I didn't want to hear the most dreadful one, which I had to eventually. The radiation oncologist drew on a piece of paper where the cancer was making its home and where it had decided to spread its wings. The back of my Warrior's nose was the base, and it had gone to put little stamps in his rib and spine. I didn't really know what to feel towards being told, "Mr Selamat, it's stage 4B nasopharyngeal cancer." Started digesting that it will be months of chemotherapy and radiation. I remembered the car ride home was deafeningly silent. I cried. He apologised.

We had to break it to the children before treatment started. We made the decision that no matter what, we were not going to hide anything from them. Transparency is important.

I spent the night just crying.

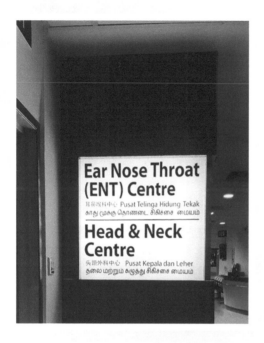

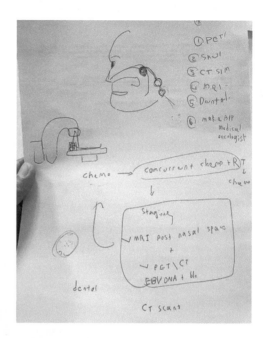

THREE

Chemo

MRI was crazy for my Warrior. He described it as being in a long tunnel, being pushed into the darkness. It felt like forever, and there seemed to be sirens so loud that it felt like he was in a construction site with lots of drilling and hacking. He also said it felt like someone firing at him with a machine gun. CT scan was not easy either. Unfortunately, over the time he was battling cancer, these became more frequent. I felt sad that he had to go through these, and I tried my best to stay calm next to him on every appointment. But it broke my heart, like it broke our hearts to have to let our five children know what was coming next in our lives. How do you break something so grave to 12-, 6-, 5-year-olds? How do you tell 2-year-old twins that their Papa can no longer carry them soon?

We told them that their Papa was sick, and during the coming weeks, they will see him get sicker as he fights this monstrous battle. The plan has been set for our Warrior to start with four cycles of chemotherapy. Each cycles have two treatments and a rest period. And then radiation therapy would start. This will all begin on 1 August 2021, a mere but daunting three weeks after being told of his illness. But as long as there was a plan, we will ride.

Amongst the appointments we had was a meet with the cancer centre's social worker. That meeting opened discussions that would otherwise be buried. I felt so relieved after that session. It was a heart-to-heart therapy. I cried, he cried, the social worker cried. A caregiver needs all the strength she could get and will feel more at ease when she actually has the resources to tap on. Emotionally, I've had time to let it sink in. Financially, it was a huge worry. Not just the medical stuff but also the daily livelihood for the seven of us. We applied for the Medifund, seeing that I will be the sole breadwinner soon.

Allah sends love when we truly need it. Our Medifund application was approved, which meant that whatever the usual Medisave and Medishield cannot sustain, Medifund would take the backfall. Just a few days before treatment began, we received out first guests. Former national service mates of my Warrior had done a "Crowdfunding for Corporal Selamat." I could not thank them enough and was ever so grateful. A little help in that avenue went a mile for a cancer family, more than anyone could imagine. A few more helps came in the coming days. I was not going to pretend that it was all fine. Our financials took a bad hit. My Warrior was a private hire driver then, and his income depended on his driving. My salary from then on became the source of stable income for the seven of us. So when help came, I was flooded with emotions and was extremely touched.

Intravenous chemotherapy promptly began on 1 August 2019. We had stepped into treatment phase. I worked from National Cancer Centre, right next to my Warrior, my life for the next two months or so. It was in the Morning Glory Suite. We were given a guide, and a nurse sat with us before it all began to explain on the process, the side effects, and what could happen. The drugs were gemcitabine and cisplatin. The first session went well. The only thing was he had to pass urine a lot of times whilst in treatments. So I was glad, as much as he was, that I'm just there to help him with it. He drove us home right after the session. In fact, for all his chemotherapy and radiation treatment that followed, my Warrior drove to the centre and back. That was how strong he was.

The side effects to chemotherapy were not only vomiting and hair loss as what we most commonly heard. My Warrior was fine on the day of chemo. He slept well. But he had a lot of hiccups and then started some spells of nauseousness, fatigue, and loss of appetite. He didn't vomit. But he slept a lot more than he usually did. Chemo also made him incredibly uncomfortable. And because we didn't have aircon back then, I was looking for air coolers to be placed in the bedroom and living area. Indeed, *rizq* can come in all shapes. A friend offered her portable aircon! Her family used it for only a couple of weeks whilst their house was getting renovated and had no use for it, so she just gave it to us in support of our quest. My workplace also gave us an air cooler. I offered to buy at a discounted price but was told to just have it.

Three days after, he lost his appetite. I ordered dates milk from a friend to sustain his diet, and it worked! He drank, albeit in small quantities. And he slept a lot.

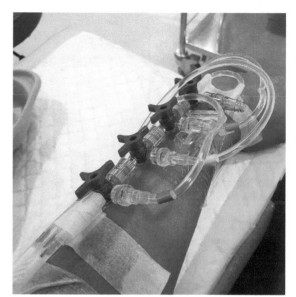

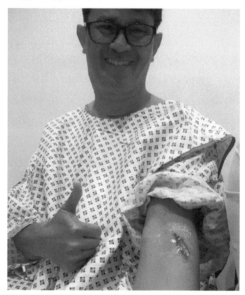

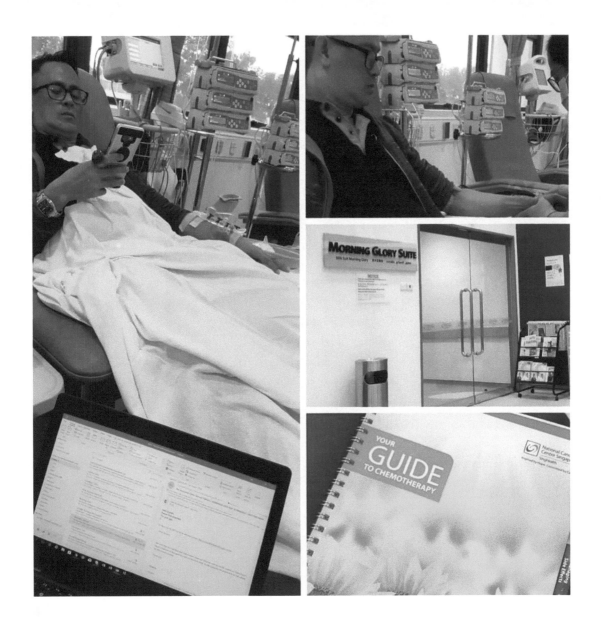

FOUR

Honeymoon

"We're going to the Maldives for our honeymoon," he said as he walked up to me, a huge smile on his face.

I couldn't believe it. He showed me the letter, and I still couldn't believe it. We're getting our house keys and will be doing some clearing up. Painting and bathrooms needed to be renovated. We're getting married in a few months, hopefully with the house ready to be moved into immediately. Maldives?!

My Warrior and I were colleagues. A week ago, our workplace had the annual dinner, and the top prize was two plane tickets on Singapore Airlines to the Maldives. Everyone was eyeing on it. In the end, the person who won it was a foreign worker. He couldn't leave Singapore for that, so my Warrior had put in an offer to buy it off. He had used his prize money for the Extra Mile Award that he won that year to get that. The full award money. He didn't think twice, all he wanted was a honeymoon that we deserve, that I deserve.

This was a second marriage for us, and he desperately wanted it to be perfect, the one that lasts, the one that will finally bring happiness, children, and beautiful memories. He wanted to start with a honeymoon that was perfect.

"I want to start the marriage by making you happy and be happy for the rest of your life with me," he said with a grin.

How can I not already be happy? This was the guy who was willing to go all out to please me. This was the guy who was tall, strong, had dimples, dark brown eyes, a deep voice, and just wants to make me happy.

We scrimped and saved to get our house ready; an intimate wedding and the honeymoon came true. We left for the Maldives three days after the wedding. Our phones were off, not even on Wi-Fi. We couldn't believe we made it there, almost one week of sun, sand, and the blue, green, and turquoise sea. Sunrise was amazing with the *adzan* being heard from the nearby local village just across Kandooma Island, where we were on. Sunsets were magical, with silhouettes that was just out of this world. With our budget, we opted for half board, meaning our hotel package had breakfast and dinner. We'll have dates at the restaurant. Lunch was also a date. At our balcony, eating cup noodles that we brought from home and freshly squeezed orange juice. Our room had the juicer and loads of oranges topped up daily. We couldn't afford the over-water villas, but we had a double-storeyed one that overlooked the beach. We watched sunsets every evening. We dressed up every night for dinner dates. We'd walked from our room to the restaurant hand in hand along the sandy and lit path. We'd be talking and giggling. We took our time with dinner. One night we even went to watch hermit crabs raced. After dinner, we'd walk back to our villa, heads looking up at the blanket of stars covering the night sky. So much beauty and awe.

"Happy?" he asked me every time we walked back.

I felt like the luckiest woman on earth. The next morning we saw a cloud shaped of a heart. It was amazing.

Instead of a ride in the catamaran, he chose to take me on a visit to the local village. The local guide picked us up, we walked around the areas hit by the Asian tsunami. My Warrior stopped to pray in a small mosque. We peeped at a school, a centre for special needs. We went on a swing and visited little shops. That's the kind of travellers we were, lots of walks. We bought a box of coasters.

As I watched him crumble to chemo side effects years later, I watched a man who just wanted to be happy and the world just failing him. How could this happen to such a wonderful guy who walked with me just to watch the stars, who would sit with me for hours just looking up at the sky?

But I knew I couldn't fumble. I had to be the strong one. I had to be the one who puts in schedules of what to do next. My man was falling, and my world was drastically changing.

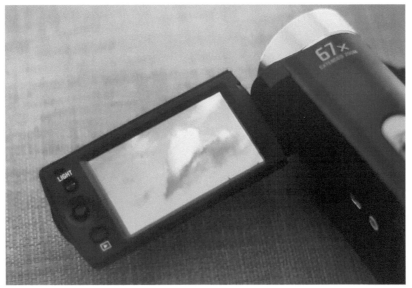

FIVE

Remedy Advises

When we announced that my Warrior was diagnosed with cancer, we had a lot of people offering alternative help. Some were subtly suggesting, some came with success stories, and some plainly pushed it to our faces. I must admit it pissed me off a couple of times. Here I was, trying to comprehend the entire situation and making the best arrangements. There they were going, "try this, try that," "give this, give that," "do this, do that." We just couldn't breathe. We knew everyone meant well, and we really did appreciate that people were thinking of us. But it was engulfing us. We did give some a try, although home remedies as these are not scientifically proven. We felt the need to try because that would be part of our efforts to keep him alive and well.

Soursop – High in antioxidants, it may help kill cancer cells, also fight bacteria, reduce inflammation, and help stabilise blood sugar levels.

My Warrior took the fruit itself, drank the tea made of boiled soursop leaves and spoonsful of the essence. He did say it energised him, plus the fruit itself was great tasting.

Roselle – Helps fight cancer cells, boost immune system, and hydrate. We made ice sticks out of roselle juice, a more fun treat for my Warrior.

Daun Belalai Gajah/Snake Grass – Supposed to help reduce swelling, treat injuries, and there are those who uses it for cancer treatment.

The leaves needed to be boiled and then drank as tea. It was not easy for my Warrior to swallow tea after tea as this was not the only things I was boiling.

Kayu Bajakah – It seemed to have the same benefits as soursop. But these are pieces of wood, which I needed to boil down to extract the essence, and the Warrior would again have it as an herbal tea. A couple of people gave us this throughout the three-year battle.

Sarang Semut/Herb Ant Nest – Supposed to halt cancer or tumour growth, helps with stiff, sore muscles and blood circulation.

After a while, the Warrior just had enough of tea after tea, especially when he was dealing with the side effects of chemo and radiation. He just wanted normalcy, drinking normal drinks.

When he was told there was no treatment anymore two years down the road, we went to see an herbalist. There were concoctions of leaves to be boiled to make tea and capsules that housed a couple of new things that we have almost never heard of.

Arjuna – It has antioxidant property that protects the heart muscles and blood vessels against damage caused by free radicals.

Curcumin – Helps reduce inflammation and prevent and treat diseases. My Warrior had this as essence and as a serum as well later in his battle. It restored his colour, so he wasn't all pale.

Cordyceps – Potentially to slow the growth of tumours and for energy.

Ashwaganda – Ancient medicinal herb that was said to reduce blood sugar levels, might have anticancer properties, reduce cortisol levels, and reduce stress.

Bee pollen – An immune booster and to increase appetite.

Apart from all these, there were other supplements. But it all came down to either being high in antioxidants or boost the immune system. These supplements were somewhat similar.

Cancer, as it is, comes in all types. One cancer patient can be a mile different from the one sitting next to him. Having people say their mother's friend took this, their neighbour's son took that, their cousin's wife ate this, and they heard people say that would help, actually, did not do much for us. We couldn't say this out because we valued their intentions. They wanted to help. They wanted to see my Warrior get well. They'll tell us every single remedy they've heard, Googled, and found. And we were grateful.

But nasopharyngeal cancer is not breast cancer, not lung cancer, not brain cancer, and not any other cancer. This is something that we generally need to understand and not generalise. My Warrior used to chat a lot about this, that it was not fair to ask if any of these made any difference after one sent us two weeks ago. We were fighting a demon that was eating my Warrior up flesh to bone, so to say.

My immediate focus was to keep him healthy enough to go through his treatments because keeping in schedule for chemo and radiation therapy was extremely important. So we started juicing. I got our elder three children involved. Arfan, who was then 12, took the lead.

My Warrior turned 50 amidst chemotherapy. His head was clean shaven as we had noticed his soft hair shedding like dry leaves. We had a surprise get-together for him for tea. We had an orange-flavoured and sprinkles birthday cake with a print of Atom Ant on it, his favourite cartoon from his childhood. We had finger food. It was a simple party, and my Warrior was immensely happy. In fact, throughout this chemo stint, we tried to incorporate the normal things when he was well enough to get up and going. We went to a wedding, he went to watch a game at the stadium, we visited Jewel, we went for drives, he sent Eshan for football training, he was working when he could, and we went for dates. Sometimes he could eat a normal meal, other times he couldn't even lift a spoon. It was filled with ups and downs.

I was proud that I could go with him and sat by his side for every chemotherapy session. The ones that lasted more than four hours and the ones that were less than two hours, I made it to all of them. I was working almost anywhere I could find a space, my laptop and me in the car, in the café, at the lounge area whilst waiting for my Warrior's turn to be called into the Jasmine or the Morning Glory Suite, next to his bedside, next to reclining chair, in between spots whilst waiting for his MRI/CT scan/shell fitting/simulation/blood tests and whilst waiting for the doctor to call him in for his check-ups. I was determined to make it work, juggling this episode and my job. I wanted to be his biggest supporter. I wanted him to know he was not doing all this alone. As much as he has always had my back, I had his as well.

When the chemo stint ended, we had about three weeks to spare before radiation therapy came in. We went for a small two-night trip into Johor Bahru, stayed at Puteri Harbour, where the kids enjoyed some long-awaited pool time and just chilling out. Happiness was ours. Moment came, and memories were created.

His recent blood tests showed that chemo was working. We were thankful to Allah. With all the stories we've heard of chemo side effects, my Warrior was rather fine. There was no severe vomiting or any major fatigue. His routine blood tests were good enough to consistently continue the treatment. None of his organs were taking a toll. Everything was on schedule. Most of the people we met said radiation therapy was a walk in the park compared to chemotherapy.

Little did we know we were about to face a scary episode.

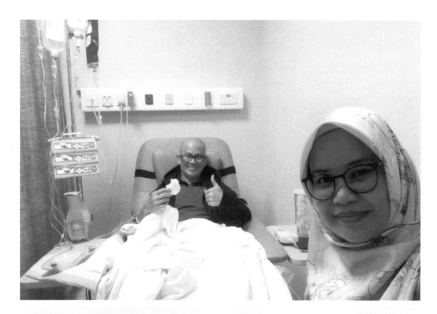

SIX

Radiation Therapy

"Let's plan a staycation. I'm well enough. Kids haven't gone anywhere since I got sick and the tests . . . the chemo. Let's take a break."

I checked our bank balance. A staycation had to be across the causeway because the rate was lower, and we could be in a bigger, better room to accommodate the seven of us. So to Johor Bahru we went. Checked out a service apartment in Puteri Harbour with the intention to just enjoy our time. We needed to get away, and the kids needed their hotel and pool time. We went for meals and walks. For three days and two nights, we were a normal family on family time.

Radiation therapy started the week after. For about a month and a half, my Warrior will need to go to the cancer centre daily, every weekday. Each session was about ten minutes, where my Warrior will need to put on his shell and lie down on a machine whilst radiation shot the targeted areas when the cancer cells were. By the end of first week, we knew it was not going to be smooth. Lots of vomiting, quite contrary to when he was in chemo. It was not easy as one of the twins was also unwell. I was cleaning puke after puke at home. I was cleaning puke halfway through replying work e-mail or dealing with some work cases. His mouth was also getting dry. He was not in the best of mood for most hours of the day.

Radiation therapy aimed at one's neck apparently will cause dry mouth. Sores could develop in the mouth and gums. Later on, as he received more therapy, he would have difficulty swallowing and stiffness in the jaw. He was already battling nausea, hair loss, giddiness, and lost appetite and taste.

There was a time when he suddenly blacked out. One moment he was walking out of our room, the next moment he was sprawled across the floor. He said, all of a sudden, everything went black for a few seconds. That was scary as we've never seen our man of the house having no control over his body. From that day on, I became extra cautious of his movement.

Sarah was graduating from kindergarten, around the same time her Papa was going through radiation therapy. I was sad that he may not be able to see her perform and snapped pictures of the graduation. But he made it. We dressed up and watched Sarah perform on stage with her class and beamed with pride as she walked up to get her certificate. And Sarah's eyes lit when she saw us in the audience. After that, Sarah came with us to the hospital for her Papa's radiation treatment for the day, face full of makeup from her performance no less. I could tell how happy she was to have her Papa see her graduate kindergarten and accompany him to the hospital. And I could also tell how relieved my Warrior was to be able to make it that day. Sarah was his princess after all.

Radiation therapy also burned his skin, around his neck and chest areas. The bigger tumours were there, neck and rib, the targeted areas of the radiation. Over time blood and pus started to appear. I could even see flesh at some parts. It was gory. The kids were really afraid to be around him, and he was so sad. He got really depressed seeing how ugly his neck was looking and that they would not go near him. Truth was, whilst the kids were afraid, they were also shocked to see the changes. They were also afraid that they might get rough and hurt him more. It got so bad that it affected his sleep. I would watch him sleep and saw him grimace and frown. Pillowcases were always stained with blood, pus, and peeling skin. I felt sad for him and was doing everything I could to ease his misery.

The hospital prescribed some cream, but it only made it worse. Plus, he was uncomfortable with the texture of the cream. We resorted to traditional means, *minyak gamat*, an ointment derived from sea cucumber known for its healing attributes. *Minyak gamat* is traditionally used to heal external pain, sprain, bloated stomach, minor cuts, skin irritation, numbness, and insect bites. So began my daily wound-cleaning duties. I would apply the ointment gently, directly onto the affected areas, yes, directly onto the blood and pus areas. This was my husband; I was willing to do anything to help him. I would then peel off the dried skin, dried blood, and whatever excess there was so the skin would heal faster.

I hid my tears as I go about the daily routine. It pained me to see him like that. It hurt me so badly to know that he was in pain. It made me so upset that he was sad to see the state he was in. But I knew the tears had to be hidden. If I wanted to help him, I had to remain the positive one, the composed one. Whilst everyone who saw him didn't bother to hide their tears, I remained straight-faced in front of them. I had to keep that composure. I could not be the one to crumble. For this wasn't just his fight but ours.

When visitors came over, we'd place a small towel over the wounds on his neck. It was not a sight for everyone. My Warrior was conscious that it might make people uncomfortable. He was also a very neat guy and didn't want anyone seeing him "improper." People used to tell him, "Never mind, we know that you're unwell." But no, he always made me check him out before he saw anyone. Sick or not, he was not going to be shabby. That was my husband, the guy I married. He always smelled good, looked clean, and had a handsome smile across his face. The bathroom smelled like a whole bottle of foam bath had been used when he stepped out of his shower. He had sprays, deodorants, *minyak attars*, lotions, and his favourite things to grab when we were at the supermarket were air fresheners for our house, for the car, and for our wardrobes. He never smelled bad a day in his life, even when with pus and blood, even towards the end of his days and he could no longer clean himself. I did everything to make sure he was all clean and smelling perfect. I put him in clean football jerseys that he loved to wear and *sarong* that matched. I would apply serum on his face, moisturiser on his arms and legs; combed his wispy hair; and then smiled at him. "Dah handsome dah, Abang." All handsome already, I would say. And he would crack a smile and told me how he appreciated that.

I missed that now, my personal time with him, getting him ready. I used to say I was the luckiest wife because my husband hugged me more than once every day whilst I helped him up from his bed, from the chair in the bathroom, from the toilet seat, and from the bed inside our room after I got him ready. Every time he needed to get up to go somewhere, he would hug me. Every time I bring him a treat, he would hug me.

Hugs. I missed his hugs. Hugs and kisses on my forehead.

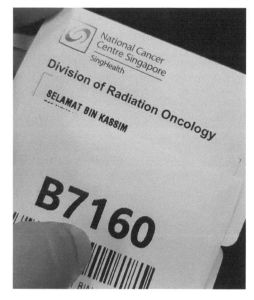

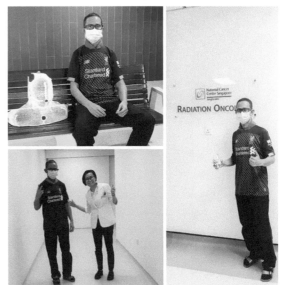

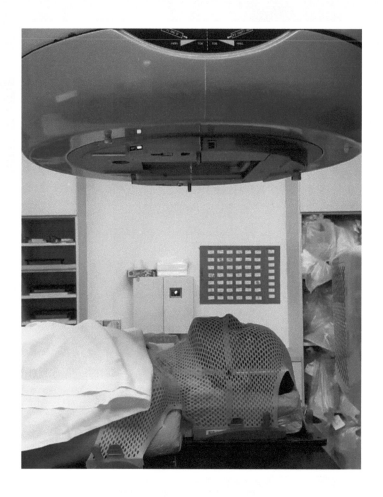

SEVEN

#theselamatentourage

Arfan came with the marriage. He was my son from a previous marriage. His father and I are on friendly terms. No messy divorce, no tussle over Arfan's care, and no financial argument. My Warrior became Arfan's Papa. Arfan was the one who decided to call him Papa, we never imposed it on him. My Warrior was so proud when Arfan first called him Papa. But step-parenting has its challenges. Arfan was five when we got married, at an age when he was just learning to have connection with his parents. And to suddenly have another father, it was confusing for Arfan. A lot of arguments happen throughout their relationship. Some are just minor, some ended in shouting banters. We anticipated that. But both were willing to learn. Both were respectful of each other. When Arfan was diagnosed with dyslexia and slow-processing skills, it broke his Papa. He took it quite hard, even though he never showed it to Arfan. He didn't want Arfan to see how upset he was because he wanted to toughen Arfan up. He was afraid that other children might bully Arfan. He was worried that Arfan would have a tough teenhood. He was very defensive when others asked about him. He never let his side of the family zoomed in on Arfan, preferring to keep Arfan away from attention. He didn't want anyone to ridicule his son. When Arfan received his PSLE results and made it to secondary school, his Papa was immensely happy and proud. He knew how hard it was for Arfan to overcome his learning challenges and came out a success. He didn't care which stream Arfan landed in; all he saw was his son was the best.

Arfan's accomplishments were his proud moments: black belt in taekwondo, knowing all the bus and MRT routes, school awards; and when Arfan came out of his shell to become a student leader, he knew that Arfan was going to be fine.

He taught Arfan how to ride a bike, to pray, to be an imam, to read, and to be a bit more street smart. Out of the five, Papa was most worried for Arfan, that people might bully him or cast him aside. He didn't really show it, but he was thankful that Arfan embraced him and then had helped him when he was unable to do anything much.

When my pregnancy test indicated a positive sign, my Warrior was the happiest person on the entire earth. Sarah was his firstborn after all. He was extremely thankful that Allah had granted his greatest wish: to have an offspring of his own flesh and blood. Sarah had the best of everything her Papa could afford. He was carrying her all the time when she was a baby. She let out a slight cry, and he'd jump out of bed. A mosquito was considered insolent for biting Sarah. Sarah's name meant princess anyway. She was her Papa's princess. Sarah could do no wrong. I used to tease him all the time that Sarah could get away with anything around Papa and the whole world would be at fault. She was his gold.

Eshan was a surprise. I was barely out of maternity leave when I found out I was pregnant again—Allah's gift. He arrived slightly less than a year after Sarah was born. Eshan's birth was long-awaited for his Papa, his biological son. Although Eshan was never treated differently than Arfan, Eshan's arrival secured his Papa's lineage. Eshan held his hopes and dreams. His Papa had a lot of plans for Eshan. He wanted to mould Eshan to be an all-rounder, one who excels his school, sports, and religion. His father-and-son moment came when Eshan started to play football at four years old. He ferried Eshan every weekend to the stadium, just to watch the preschooler run around in the field. When there was an end-season football carnival at the national stadium, his excitement was as if Eshan was going to play for the national team. "My son is going to be a football star," he said. He wanted to take Eshan to watch matches at the stadium. He was looking forward to staying up to watch matches on TV when Eshan was old enough to stay up: World Cup, Euro, Premier League, any leagues. He dreamed of travelling on a football tour with Eshan. "One day I want to take Eshan to Anfield," home of his favourite Liverpool football team.

He said, "I also want Eshan to be an Ustaz," a religious scholar. He wanted Eshan to be the best in religion amongst his siblings. It was a need to him. There must be a boy in the family who is the strongest in religion, the one who will keep the others in check. He didn't want to impose it on Arfan because of his learning challenges, and Eshan was his only biological son. Eshan held the most of his hopes and dreams.

Just when we thought we were done with babies, after all I was already thirty-five by then, it was positive on the test kit once again. The pregnancy was confirmed just before Hari Raya that year. And on Hari Raya, my Warrior was announcing to everyone that we were going to have another baby soon. Little did we know we were expecting twins! When people commented how much Sarah and Eshan were like twins because of their close age and being similar in size, my Warrior had taken it as a prayer.

"Let them," he said. "Who knows, what they said turned to prayers and Allah will grant us real twins? Wouldn't that be lovely?" He grinned.

"Okay, I see two baby heartbeats," the words of the sonographer at KKH.

"Alhamdulillah," the words of my Warrior, thanking Allah for the blessing.

I was speechless. I couldn't believe what I just heard and seen on screen. I looked at my Warrior and he was so happy. The smile never left him for the rest of the day.

The pregnancy was tough, lots of appointments as they were considered high-risk because of my age and they were sharing a placenta. Plus, I've had three caesarean sections prior. When we found out they were identical girls, the Warrior was telling the entire world.

The girls had to be delivered earlier than planned in an emergency as I was hit with Bell's Palsy and somehow had a lot of contractions. Naela spent about two weeks in the hospital, whilst the younger-by-one-minute Nadra was able to come home with us. Life was hectic with twin infants, a three-year-old, a four-year-old, and a ten-year-old. But I was blessed with a hands-on husband. He took over the elder three so I could concentrate on the early days with the twins. He was up at night with me, even though he had a habit of placing the babies in the wrong cots and confusing me after that on which ones I had fed. Luckily, we had put them in different coloured clothes. My Warrior would put them to sleep as well after I fed them so I can catch like ten minutes of sleep before the other woke up for her feed. The early days were difficult and tiring and costly. But it was eased because I had a husband who was supportive and attentive. The day Naela and Nadra entered infant care, my Warrior took me out on a date. He knew it was a day to celebrate being out, without mommy duties. It was hilarious that we actually enjoyed being away from our own children, almost vulgar for some people. But if you have been all-hands-aboard parents like us, you will live for these dates.

The five of them were my Warrior's pride and joy. He updated on his Instagram, he sent pictures to his friends, and he talked about them all the time. Everything they did amused him. He couldn't believe that in his 40s, Allah finally granted his lifelong prayer with not just one but four biological children and one gifted child and a great mix of boys, girls, and twins! He thanked me all the time for being okay to have that many children. I didn't even think I wanted this many children. But I was confident because he was confident.

I was even confident enough for us to travel on a plane. Imagine just us with five kids in a plane to Medan and then long road trips to stay in the highlands overlooking Lake Toba, taking a local ferry to an island, and just being in foreign land. I was confident because I knew I have a great partnership with my Warrior.

We went for a lot of road trips into several places in Johor, Melaka, Selangor, and staycations. We took a ferry for our Batam vacation. Stroller, carriers, and whatever we need to travel, we brought along, from the time we only had Arfan 'til the time there were seven of us. We travelled. We went to Bandung and Bali when we only had three children. Sarah broke her arm in Bali, and yet it never unfazed us to just travel with children. It was something we wanted to do—to let the children see the world more than we had. We even planned that someday we'd take them all to the same island we were on in the Maldives because which child wouldn't like sun, sand, and sea all day long? We were raising them to love being outdoors. Our day-outs were usually being in open spaces, where the children could run, outdoor playgrounds, the beach, and was rarely malls and enclosed spaces.

It was the children and us doing things together. Never mind the hassle, the tantrums, and the craziness.

We were most worried about how the children would react when they saw their Papa get sick and sicker. So we made the decision to be open with them. Nothing should be hidden and that they should hear from us first before they get their own ideas on the situation or, worse, hear it from someone else. We figured being truthful and upfront will benefit us all than hiding facts. So throughout the three years that their Papa was fighting cancer, we sat down and talked a couple of times. The diagnosis, the side effects, the situation at that moment, what the doctors were doing, and when there was no more treatment, we let them in on what was to be expected as well. Of course, we need to trust in Allah's plans. Most times we felt like the children took every news perfectly, even proving us wrong. But it didn't take the sunken feeling that the children were not having a normal childhood.

Our hearts broke thinking of that.

EIGHT

2020

In January 2020, we went for a review with the radiation oncologist. Before that, we had gone on our annual year-end staycation to Johor Bahru. We thought we were not going to be able to, but we did! We had the most gorgeous large suite that had a huge outdoor patio and an awesome view. It was to celebrate the end of his arduous treatments as well. The radiation scars were still there, so he always had a towel draped around his neck. Believe it or not, he drove for this trip across the causeway. That was how strong-willed he was.

My Warrior was not in the clear, but there was progress. The treatment had successfully decreased the cancer cell count, but more blood tests were needed. If it further decreased, great. If it remained stagnant or showed signs of increase, we would need to see if we could wait a bit more or another round of chemo to start again. When we told family and friends, they asked about the stage again. Here's the thing: The stage 1 diagnosis will not change just because some treatment could have worked. It remained a stage 4. But we took comfort that his hair was growing, weight was slowly climbing as his appetite slowly grew, and scars were disappearing. He was also back to chatting on the phone more, and his bad jokes were making a comeback. My Warrior was back to normal.

He was still taking soft diet for most times, but his taste buds were coming to life. And we couldn't be more excited because my Warrior was such a foodie. He was my food buddy, and I was so happy to have him back. Slowly, he was able to take in his favourite foods again.

In February 2020, it was review day again. A scan was done a week before. Allah knew how much I had lost sleep over that day. The scan showed the primary tumour that was at the back of his nose and the ones at his neck were gone. The treatment worked! Praise to Allah. However, the scan also detected new tumours on his spine. It was looking like the cancer was travelling down the bone. It was on his L5, where he had his non-cancer-related surgery seven years ago. The options given to us were live with cancer or new cycles of chemotherapy. There was no way we could kill off the cancer, we had to accept that tumours will just pop up, and we would then need to deal with it as best we could. I read "palliative" in the letter. And I knew what it was. We could now only try to relieve; the cancer cannot be cured.

Metastasis – The spread of cancer cells to new areas of the body by way of bloodstream or lymphatic system.

Plainly put, tumour decided to set up camp elsewhere.

I went on a breakdown that week. Having a husband with Stage 4 cancer was not like having an adult son with cancer. Or a brother with cancer. Or a friend with cancer. Or a parent with cancer. Or a neighbour with cancer. Or an in-law with cancer. Or a best buddy with cancer. Or a role model with cancer. Or a schoolmate with cancer. Or a colleague with cancer. This is the guy I fell in love with, the one who swept me off my feet with butterflies in my tummy whenever he rang. The one I had hopes and dreams with as I took his hand in marriage. The one whom I shared many great happy and sad stuff behind closed doors. The one who laughed at my most unfunny jokes to say the least. The one whom I had hoped to protect and love me all my life. The one who caught me when I fell. Literally. The one who held up my hair when I wanted to vomit, visually not very attractive. Each person in your life is there for various but very different reasons. No one is the same. I had wished the people who tried to coax us not try to find similarities. That was just horrible. And I was also not in the mood to discuss future.

And then Covid-19 hit the entire world.

Sometime in March 2022, we had a medical emergency. Because of drastic weight changes when the Warrior was having treatment, he developed hernia. We were supposed to schedule a surgery, but it became urgent when he was really in pain. Because of Covid, only one visitor was allowed. So I was running around, from the house to the hospital, for a couple of days. We were fortunate that Sengkang General Hospital was only a ten-minute bus ride. It meant I could go for visits and still be home with the children quickly.

Because of Covid, the children were at home. It also meant that I was unable to accompany my Warrior for his treatments. And that was a sore time in my life. I wanted to be there so badly. In May 2020, the preparation began again, starting with MRI. My Warrior drove and went for each treatment alone. It saddened me immensely. I was working at home and tending to children on homebased learning, whilst my Warrior was managing it all by himself at the cancer centre.

Before radiation therapy began, my Warrior had asked for *Ketam Kari Asam*. It's crab fried in curry paste with tamarind, his favourite, and I did it. My Warrior loved crabs. So did I.

Radiation therapy to the L5 began in June 2020. That was the second season of radiation therapy after the more intensive one in 2019. I was so nervous for him and was praying that this time around, it would not be as painful. It was just for very few sessions and the side effects were not as bad.

But we were tested once again, this time of a different nature.

Sarah and I were in the car driven by my Warrior on the way to my sister's place when we met with a road accident. My sister had just given birth a few weeks back, and we were on the way to meet the baby. At square junction, the driver of a car coming from our left had beat the red light and crashed onto us. It was terrifying! Our car was spun after the bang and almost hit an incoming bus from the opposite direction. My Warrior sustained injury to the wrist because of the hard control on the steering wheel. I had injury to my legs, one had to be cast and then was in an air boot for a couple of months. Sarah, by Allah's grace, did not sustain any injury. But she was visibly shocked, and we were amazed at how well she was handling it over the next few days.

That incident was giving me restless nights. For a while, I refused to be in a car. And when I was, I refused to sit in the front seat. I also refused to watch the video of the incident. Some other drivers had uploaded the accident from their own dashcams. It was a close shave. I was also uneasy when any vehicle got too close to the car I was in.

The case was handed over to the lawyers because of some complication over that driver's side. My Warrior left this world without ever knowing what the outcome of the case was. Two years on and we have yet to get any closure.

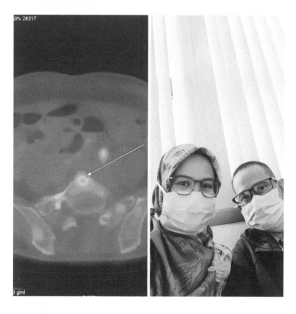

NINE

One-Year Strong

In July 2020, we marked my Warrior's one-year strong. He has gone into battle for one year. It had been tough, but he powered on. Apart from his difficulty to breakdown food in his mouth, everything was normal. Radiation had, in the long run, given him dry mouth issues. Later he went on to have difficulty chewing and swallowing. Sometime in July, he managed to finish a full rib-eye steak, another one of his favourite food. I remembered we took Arfan and Sarah out to Elfuego at Jewel, and my Warrior ordered a rib-eye. The other three children were at the childcare centre. My Warrior was so excited about it, and when the steak arrived, he slowly ate it. We waited for him as he chewed more than average times the small pieces of meat that he cut. He loved it, and I felt like crying for joy when he finished it. It has been a while since he wiped out a plate like that. Cancer-fighting was what my Warrior did, not for a living but to live. And these were the triumphs that we rallied for and celebrated.

In August, there was another review. The tumour at the spine was gone. *Alhamdulillah.* The radiation therapy had managed to hit the spot. But of course, there was a *but*. A new "camp" was detected at his right rib. There was no break. Because radiation cannot be done too close to the last one, the oncologist suggested oral chemo, meaning he had to take medication twice a day. He was put on trial for three weeks for the first cycle, and then they will review if they can continue. This was the tumour that eventually turned nasty and set up its camp to many other spots in my Warrior's body. This was the tumour that made him miserable for the next two years of his life, the cause of all his pain.

45

Despite that, we marked another milestone. He turned 51. At 51, he looked much better than when he was 50. He didn't look ill. No one would know what he has stage 4 cancer if they never asked. He was working longer hours. He was eating well. He was perfect.

We brought out his grill and had an assortment of barbequed stuff for his birthday gathering. He was the grill master. We had *Durian Serawa* cake. We had a lot of laughter, too much to eat, and for that moment, forgot that he was on oral chemo. If there was one thing we learned from our Warrior having cancer was to live life as it is.

The side effects of oral chemo were minor, fatigue and lack of appetite. This went on for two to three months before it was time for the next scan to see if the treatment worked.

In October 2020, it looked as though the tumour at the rib was leaving. It didn't leave yet, though, just showing signs of shrinking. However, the blood tests showed the EB virus that caused the cancer was on the rise. And that was worrying. My Warrior was given two options: intravenous chemo again or continue with the oral chemo. He chose oral chemo, only because he was more comfortable with taking medication. And oral chemo would allow him to be more himself and continue driving. I supported his decision. After all, it was his body, and he was the one going through it. I took it as he knows what was best for himself.

In November 2020, there were no visible tumours in my Warrior's body. However, blood tests were showing the EB virus to be rising. What it meant was the cancer cells were somewhere around but could not be clearly detected. We were looking at "invisible spots." The doctors were puzzled because my Warrior appeared healthy and unaffected, but the number was alarming. They scheduled him for six months of weekly intravenous chemo.

Now one may argue that we should not have agreed to the chemo since my Warrior appeared healthy. Why ruin it? We should have just gone on with our daily lives. After all, chemo could also kill off healthy cells. I did have that thought. But we needed to try every possibility. My Warrior was thinking of his children. Arfan was 13, Sarah was 7, Eshan was 6, and the twins were only 3. He felt the need to try because he wanted a fair chance of seeing them grow up.

It was a tearful night as we talk things through and came to a decision. In December 2020, the chemo began. As it turned out, that was the final chemotherapy my Warrior had to go through.

I worked from Starbucks near the cancer centre or at home. As most sessions were in the morning and it could run for hours, my Warrior drove himself home after each session as I needed to pick Sarah up from school at midday. A new battle has begun, in a war that had seen nothing short of resilience.

Alhamdulillah

Today, marks 1 year since my Warrior was officially diagnosed & started his cancer-fighting journey. One Year Strong.

TEN

Medan

March 2018. We didn't have a lot that year. We just finished paying off our monthly instalments for the twins' birth. And having twins did mean two times of everything. We struggled through the diaper, milk, clothes, and whatever baby needs there was. But we wanted to take the kids somewhere and as with the other children, wanted to fly at least once whilst Naela and Nadra were within the age to fly for free. So wherever we planned to go needed to fulfil certain criteria: cheap flight tickets, affordable itinerary and hotel, somewhere new and we've never been before, kid-friendly, and during the March school holidays. We decided on Medan, Indonesia.

The flight was short enough for Naela and Nadra to get their first experience. Arfan's first was to Manila, Philippines. Sarah's was Bandung, Indonesia, whilst I was pregnant with Eshan, and Eshan's was Bali, Indonesia. Naela sat on her Papa's lap for the flight.

We booked a local land package, so we were picked up from the airport and then a long road trip from Kualanamu Airport to Lake Toba in Northern Sumatra. It was so beautiful to be on the highlands.

Travelling with children obviously came with all sorts of colour. There were mood swings, whining, squabbles, crying, plainly misbehaving, multiple toilet breaks, and mishap. There were also laughter, smiles, excitement, hugs, and awe. And we handled it all—together. Never once was I left to do things on my own. My Warrior was a very hands-on father, he got involved in anything and everything that I needed to get the family going. He woke up in the middle of the night after a tiring day of travelling for the twins' milk feeds. When we needed to change diapers midway, he made sure that if I was doing it that he got the others. I wouldn't have had the confidence to bring toddlers and preschoolers up to the mountains if it wasn't him being my partner.

On the first night, we slept 906m above sea level. The next day we were on a road trip again, even went on a local ferry ride to Samosir Island for sightseeing. All the time when we're walking around, I had one baby strapped to my chest in a carrier, and my Warrior had the other. When it's feeding time, my Warrior will take one as well. He helped me get all the children ready for our itinerary. It was a partnership, a successful one. We never had issues when we travel that we couldn't handle together.

The kids rode on horses, went to fruit market, hike up hills, saw volcanoes and waterfalls, ate durians at a local village, hung out by Lake Toba, enjoyed running about the cold outdoors, visited a palace, ate local meals, had tea in the highlands, went shopping for souvenirs, loads of sightseeing, went on local ferry on Lake Toba, stopped by local bakery, and had lots of walking.

I remembered I had miscalculated on the amount of milk formula that I packed for the twins. Or perhaps the higher altitude was making them drink more. We ran out by day 3. My Warrior settled us into the hotel before setting off on foot to the supermarket to look for a pack. Never once did he put the blame on me. One thing with my Warrior was he always trusts that I would have done my best, and there was no need to get frustrated on these little things. He got a local brand, and we prayed that the twins would not reject it. We watched in anticipation as they gulped down their bottles 'til the last drop. We celebrated the triumph and were thankful that we had easy babies to feed.

The same went to other children as well. Whatever was served to them whilst we were on vacation, they would just have them. Of course, we had made sure the food was suitable for them. But not once did we have a complete rejection that we needed to hunt for other food. My Warrior was also not one who was picky with food. He'd try almost anything. He'd be thankful for the simplest of food and grateful for the most extravagant. He was the one who made me eat foods I would've otherwise stayed away, except cheese. He didn't succeed in that one.

His easy-going nature when it comes to food, as long as it is *halal*, had passed down to his wife and children. Arfan, who wouldn't touch traditional and spicy Malay cuisines, now would devour them and go for seconds. Eshan has a penchant for durians, nuts, unagi, and *malay kuihs*, just like his Papa. Sarah loves Japanese food. Naela has an appetite that rivalled her Papa when he was healthy. Nadra loves snacking, just like her Papa. But she'll also eat her greens and fruits, just like her Papa.

We came home from the trip extremely tired but equally happy. Sure there were meltdowns and yelling. Sure we didn't get that much rest or even sleep through the night. Sure we may have burst the budget. But we were so thankful for the experience.

It turned out to be Naela and Nadra's first plane trip and only plane trip with their Papa. We never got to fly again with the children after that. The Warrior was diagnosed with cancer the following year, and Covid engulfed the entire world soon after. When he was fine for travel in 2020, the borders were all closed. No flying was possible.

My Warrior had always spoke about that trip with happiness and sadness. He wished he could have travelled more, especially with Naela and Nadra. He was sad that the twins had very little vacations with him compared to their siblings. But there was nothing much he could do, and they had a few vacations with him, road trips and via ferry to a resort in Batam, Indonesia. We also squeezed in two staycations in Singapore when my Warrior was terminal but could still walk. We tried. We wanted the children to know that we really tried to get as much family experience as possible as the seven of us.

Live for the moments and don't hesitate.

ELEVEN

Those Six Months

It was Eshan's turn to graduate kindergarten that December. Since there was Covid restriction, graduation pictures were not taken in school. Instead, we were asked to make an appointment with the childcare centre's designated photographer for a slot at the studio. We decided to make it a family affair. We all dressed up and took pictures as a family with Eshan in his graduation attire.

"I don't know if I'll see any of our kids graduate for real," my Warrior had said. "At least we will have this one picture for treasure."

I felt a lump in my throat and an uneasy feeling in my stomach.

The children had fun at the photoshoot. We've never had a photoshoot at the studio. We had picture as a family taken, all seven of us. We also had pictures of just the children and of just Eshan, the main man.

As the studio was in Woodlands, my Warrior drove us all to the waterfront right after. The waterfront overlooked Johor Bahru, Malaysia.

"So near yet so far. I wonder if we'll ever have another vacation there." My Warrior stood facing the neighbouring country. "This Covid thing is really ruining it for us."

On 16 December 2020, the second journey through intravenous chemotherapy started, six cycles this time. Each cycle has three sessions, once a week and one rest week. The aim was to keep my Warrior well enough to go through all six cycles within six months. We prayed that he wouldn't catch Covid or any other infections and viruses. We prayed for the side effects to be manageable. We prayed that this would work, even though we knew chances were extremely slim.

I couldn't be at the treatment suite like I did in 2019 because of Covid restrictions. I wasn't happy. I was afraid that my Warrior would think he had to do it alone. I was his supporter, his cheerleader, and his wall to let off frustrations. I sent him to the NCC's doorstep and made my way to Starbucks which was at the next building. I set up my office there and waited anxiously for updates.

He came out fine. We went to get his head shaved after that. We saw how his hair fall during the first journey, and to block that from happening, we welcomed the Jason Statham style once again.

Fatigue and mood swings soon take position. It was tough but manageable. There were days when all my Warrior wanted to do was sleep. And when he wasn't sleeping, he'd pick an argument over almost anything. On most times, I would dismiss it as a side effect. On other times, it would turn into a major argument because I was tired from juggling everything in our house and family. I needed to tell him that what he was doing or saying was wrong, especially when he started to find faults with the children, scolding them for little errors, yelling at them for making noise and throwing things around. Chemotherapy was nasty physically and mentally. He would say things out of ordinary and at times hurtful. Whilst I wanted the children to understand, which they usually do, I also had to be fair to them. There was a limit as to what the children could comprehend and take in. And we were dealing with children of different age groups. I had to, unfortunately, step in and took sides. It was horrible because I never wanted anyone to feel that they were lesser than the other. And I also did not want them to think that it was always Papa against them. Taking sides took a toll on me. I was left completely exhausted after every episode. And there was always someone in the house who didn't like what I did or said. Motherhood was already difficult as it is. Top it with caregiving, I didn't even know what to think sometimes. So I ended up taking the blame.

My Warrior would eventually apologise when he cooled off, sometimes tearful as he didn't know what got to him. He'd hug me and said he loved me. He loved us a lot. If he wasn't ill and having all those drugs in his body, my Warrior was a funny, cheerful and easy-going person. He loved making us happy, even 'til his last.

By early 2021, there seemed to be a typical pattern on most days. My Warrior would be all fine, walking and laughing for a couple of hours. And then the side effects of chemotherapy knocked him double over. And it's a rapid drop in physical strength, succumbing to muscle aches, facial numbness, and body pains from no exact source. There was one time I actually took pictures of this change. He had driven us to Arab Street area that morning. At 11:00 a.m. he was pushing Sarah and Eshan on the swings. We hung out at a café at noon, had lunch at close to 2pm. We walked around in between and after. All the time, he was active, laughing, joking around, and shopping a little. At 7:30 p.m., he was knocked out. He didn't even want dinner. And he slept 'til the next morning.

Whilst he was asleep, Sarah asked, "Why does Papa have cancer?"

That was tough. To see her Papa's energy suddenly slide was difficult for her to comprehend. She was eight after all. She saw her Papa woke up and did the usuals. Her mind was at peace, everything was all right, and then came the slide, and she got worried. That question needed to be handled delicately.

This chemo cycle, because it was spaced apart, there were days that my Warrior would take me out on breakfast dates after we dropped the kids at school. Breakfast dates were precious. It was the only time we can have a meal outside, just the two of us. We loved our breakfast dates, and we went as often as we could. When all the kids were in school, it was good to reconnect and be the individuals that we were, talking adult stuff or just joking around being silly, away from the yelling, tired, and crazy parents that we were most of the week, away from my laptop of back-to-back cases. It could be a simple *prata* at Jalan Kayu or *appom* at Tekka Market or a full set at Dutch Colony or *kacang pool* at Geylang Serai. Anywhere, we made breakfast dates our thing.

Cycle five of chemotherapy was during Ramadan, our fasting season. My Warrior decided he wanted to carry on fasting as well. I was worried, but I also wanted to support him. And I thought how noble he was. He still wanted to do all the religious obligations despite his condition. He did his five prayers. He had the Quran verses read around the house daily. He watched Islamic forums on screen. He asked the appropriate people for advice. He did the core and a bit more. He cried after every prayer, asking Allah to help and guide him. Our religion was his strength. *Maghrib* was, as much as he could, a congregational in our house. He thought Arfan and Eshan to be imams. He was preparing them.

He always said, "Jangan tinggal solat." Never miss a prayer.

So he fasted and completed his fast. A man with stage 4 cancer and going through chemotherapy was fasting—talk about pure strength and determination! We didn't need to look far for inspiration, just take a good look at our Warrior. We lived with a Warrior.

We had a quiet wedding anniversary in May that year. It was during Ramadan. When we got married, we never promised the world because look at the world, Covid-filled. Who'd want to promise that? We never promised all will be okay because all will never be okay until we reached Jannah with Allah's will. We never promised wealth and richness because wouldn't we be resentful of each other then? But we promised to always have each other's back and walk in our own shoes. And we did 'til his end.

The anniversary date was also an appointment date at the cancer centre. It was with his oncologist. We were hoping that he would be fine to move his chemo date a bit to accommodate Hari Raya celebrations so he could help around and enjoy the festivities, instead of being plagued with extreme fatigue whilst dealing with side effects. I could accompany my Warrior for the appointment that afternoon as Arfan had come home from school earlier and agreed to babysit Sarah and Eshan. The twins were at childcare. Arfan, at 14, was more independent than peers of that age. He grew up a lot faster with his life experiences. For that, I have always been thankful. For that, his Papa has always been proud. He'd tell everyone how Arfan did so many things around the house when he couldn't. He'd gushed over how Arfan had always surprised him with the things he could do. But they were almost always at loggerheads. Arfan wanted his Papa to see his point. His Papa wanted Arfan to take steps back and see the bigger picture, to be respectful of elders, and to think before he spoke. But they respected each other. And that was the most important.

We were granted the change in dates for the last cycle of chemo. We had a wonderful, normal Hari Raya. There were still Covid restrictions, so we didn't quite visit anyone. But we had guests coming over, and we entertained. We spent time as a family through the festivities. I cooked all the usual festive dishes that he loved, the spicy ones. Turned out that was the last time my Warrior could take spicy food for Hari Raya.

My Warrior rang the bell at the cancer centre on 10 June 2021. Ringing the bell signified the end of chemotherapy. Cancer patients would know what it felt like. For some, a brand new chapter awaits. For others, uncertainty or that was it. His was the latter.

TWELVE

"It's six months to a year, Mrs Selamat."

We celebrated Father's Day and end of chemo that weekend. I wanted to let our Warrior know that we love and support him, no matter what. My friend, Netty, baked the most delicious brownie that she left uncut so it looked like a big cake. The children and I decorated it with superhero cake toppers. He was our superhero. We live with a superhero, a Warrior. How many of us could say that? My mother made *roti kirai*. Arfan and I did our own homemade shell-out because our Warrior loved seafood. It was a wonderful celebration.

On 22 June 2021, we went for a review at the cancer centre. We were edgy. I couldn't sleep the night before. I wasn't in the mood to talk the entire journey there.

The oncologist classified his cancer as a "stable disease," meaning, it was not going away, and the EBV reading had not really gone down to as low as they had hoped. But the spots detected were contained, not growing in size or showing signs of spreading. His organs remained unaffected, and the blood count was good. There was nothing much we could do at that point but to watch. The oncologist then gave my Warrior a ten-week break from any form of treatment. We accepted, and by then, we were working through traditional and herbal means to keep the cancer at bay. We prayed and prayed for the best.

That July, we passed through the second anniversary of my Warrior's battle with this nasty cancer. The second year was filled with more emotional roller coaster, enlightenment, and knowledge than the first. My Warrior was not out of the woods and was probably would never be. But we lived knowing that each day counted, each moment lasted, and each memory cast. There are things worth fighting for and so many not even worth a minute of worry. Our trust in Allah only remained deep.

Take more pictures.
Always say "I love you."
Never go to bed mad.
Jump first, think second.
Love harder, love deeper.
Life is just too short.

Ten weeks passed. And so the story went on how a beginning filled with aspiration came to a juncture on 1 September 2021.

"What is the life expectancy we're looking at here?" This wife had to ask the doctor in front of her, composed.

My heart was just breaking. I had asked a question that I had hoped I never had to ask. But I had to, at least in the educated calculation of man. What Allah had planned, we didn't know. After that ten-week wait-and-see, the tumours decided to grow and spread at a rate that doctor had regretfully brought up palliative care. There was another option, another form of chemo with only 15% chance and a possibility of organs being affected. My Warrior's body simply could not be up for it.

"It's six months to a year, Mrs Selamat."

The doctor left the room to let us have a moment. I remembered that tearful conversation.

"I'm done, Dinda," my Warrior started. "This is all I can do."

"Do you not want to see Naela and Nadra go into primary 1? Or Sarah and Eshan growing up? Or Arfan be an adult?" I cried.

I was in denial and actually hung on to that 15%. To me, a chance is a chance, a path to walk, sprint, jump, and whatever it needed to get through. I wasn't ready for him to throw the towel.

"A 15% chance, Dinda? And to ruin the parts that are doing just fine? My heart is fine, my lungs are good, my kidneys are working, my brain is still sane. I don't want to ruin them. And I want to be at peace. I want the quality of life whilst I still can. This is it. We've tried for over two years, and I am tired." He looked at my tearful face, held my hands, and said, "I love you. You'll be okay."

After a few moments, the doctor walked in on me just trying to gain back some kind of composure, really. My Warrior told him what he decided. After two years of nonstop battle, the path was now to let nature take its course. The trust in Allah was even deeper.

I was just a teary wreck from then on and for a couple of days after. I went from sad to angry to just wanting to be left alone. I had remained positive for two years, and this wasn't easy for me to just digest. I was nervous, anxious, and annoyed at the same time.

We announced it to our circles, and some questions left me wanting to swing Thor's hammer. But for some, showers of concerns and love, messages, DMs, and visits. A lovely couple even brought us groceries. We've had a few offers to get supplements, with some bringing them over and a few were ordered for the Warrior. We even had some plants delivered, apparently for medicinal value. Those leaves I had to dry and boil to make tea. Everyone wanted to see him well. This chapter of his cancer journey was our pledge of not wanting him to give up, for him to remain positive, to have the strength and, most importantly, faith.

That weekend we took the children for a morning picnic by the beach. We set up our portable table, laid out some packed food, and just enjoyed the morning out. My Warrior pitched the portable goal post and spent some time running around, playing football with Eshan. That was extremely precious. The girls played sand, and so did Arfan. Lots of laughter that morning. We took pictures of that day, and we knew that these moments will be fleeting soon.

We took the children out as much as we could. One time we went on a playground tour. My Warrior drove to an Alice in Wonderland-themed playground and then to larger playground with an amazing long train and sandpit. We had finger food for dinner right by the playground. After which, my Warrior drove us to Gardens by the Bay to enjoy the Lantern Festival exhibits. We ended the night with ice creams at East Coast Park. We had a ton of fun. The children were extremely happy; one was because the Covid restrictions had somewhat relaxed a little, and being out in a group of seven like us was somewhat normal again. My Warrior wanted the kids to see that we could enjoy a day-out with minimal cost and that the outdoors were the best. He knew his body will crumble and wanted to do as much as he could with his children. I ended up planning outings that were on small budget. Our money was running low, and it worried me day and night. We prayed for sustenance.

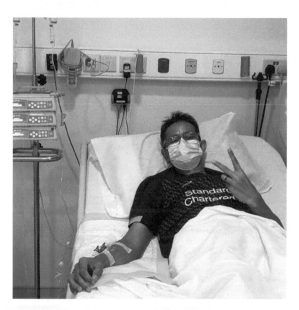
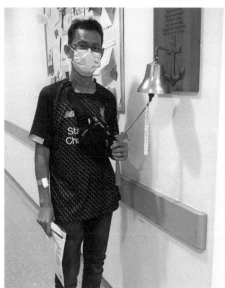

THIRTEEN

Bank, Drones, and Darts

The moment I knew my Warrior had cancer, one of my biggest worries was our finances. We will be surviving on one income. And for a family of seven, it's a stretch.

I applied for aids that we could be allowed to get, the main thing being the children's education and my Warrior's medical. I figured those are the most important ones.

Lots of paperwork to fill up, and I dutifully did them all. The key to getting subsidies and aids is to be as open as possible. Complete the paperwork and be upfront.

For the twins, they attend Sparkletots childcare. Sarah and Eshan did too. Their principal was the first to offer her assistance to obtain maximum subsidies. When I told her about the situation we were in, she immediately applied what she could to assist. The last thing she wanted me to worry were the children's childcare fees. We succeeded in obtaining the maximum subsidy possible, and that was a huge load off my back. There was to be no more cash top-ups involved as the children had enough in their CDA (child development account) to sustain their preschool education.

And when Sarah and Eshan finally entered primary school, we applied for MOE FAS (Ministry of Education Financial Assistance Scheme), together with Arfan. With Allah's will, they got approved. It helped us with the expenses for their school uniforms, books, transport allowance, and daily canteen expenditure.

For my Warrior's medical, we applied for Medifund. This was done way ahead through the cancer centre's social worker, and it was a yearly-renewal scheme that went into place should my Warrior's Medisave or Medishield were exhausted. We were fortunate and immensely thankful that throughout the three-year fight, we didn't need to come up with any cash to pay for the treatments or the medication. That took a huge chunk of worry off our plates.

When all those were approved, we tried to supplement our daily expenditure and commitments with our own salary. We also had wonderful family, friends, and neighbours who came by and gifted us with some cash. We used those to tide things over.

Because of the Covid situation, I had a salary cut for six months. I felt the need to do something to make up for the shortage. So my Warrior and I started to dabble in dropship and being agents for some items that we could sell and make some profit. It was our little project, and we enjoyed the run.

The rest, we depended on our own savings. However, we never felt that things were not enough. Somehow we could afford to have the things we need and want. With Allah's will, we were always sustained. That, to us, was a miracle itself.

A couple of people around us suggested that we appeal for more assistance. Perhaps for groceries and pocket money. But we just felt that there are more deserving families that should get those. A lot of families in Singapore with ill members need help and at times didn't know where to begin. Perhaps because they have never heard of such bodies or are uncomfortable to come forward. Others could be because of the lengthy process and paperwork to get them. Or perhaps too invasive. In the end, finances became a pressure. And that is sad.

I felt the need to keep my job at all costs. No matter how busy I got with caregiving, this family needed that income. My Warrior was driving lesser and lesser. I didn't think he should be driving for a living anymore either. I was worried for his safety. He, on the other hand, wanted to do a lot with whatever little time and strength he had.

He cultivated a new hobby to relieve stress and tiredness. Imagine living your end of life and you still wanted a new hobby. That was my Warrior. He learned how to pilot drones more than five years ago when he signed up for a basic course. He wanted a switch of careers then and be a photographer or a surveyor using drone. But that would mean that he needed to go for more advanced courses, which he couldn't afford. So he shelved that knowledge and brought it out again. He ordered some new drones, which he had a budget for, and started flying them again, watched YouTube videos to better himself. So his routine became send the children to school, work a while, and find spots to fly his drone. Occasionally, I tagged along. The joy he got from flying the drones was a delight to watch. He beamed with such happiness when he watched the videos he recorded from the drone.

"I got my eye in the sky," he said with a smile.

We loved his drone shots and his stories for the day, of where he went to fly them, of how he nearly smashed it to a tree once and almost lost one in the waters. He loved what he did, and I loved it when he was excited and happy.

When he couldn't move much later on, flying drones was something he sadly missed. I was sad for him too. It was one of the last activities he did, that and playing darts.

To get his movement at home in check, he fixed a dartboard up and got some darts, just for him to throw for fun. He enjoyed it when those who came for a visit would get into a game with him. It was a simple thing, yet it brought him so much joy. I entertained him at darts when he wanted to play late at night. I remembered being so tired yet still entertaining him. I remembered not understanding the game or where exactly I should be aiming, yet I played anyway because I wanted to see him smile. Sometimes he'd be at the dart board when he couldn't sleep. I'd hear it from the bedroom.

Two days before his passing, a few family members came over to celebrate Hari Raya Haji with us. My Warrior was, by then, in his bed most of the time. He heard a few of them playing his darts.

"Would you like to watch?" I asked him, and he nodded.

I helped him up and sat him on his commode chair, wheeled him nearer to the dart space, and he watched them play. He was happy, even though he asked to be put back in his bed after ten minutes. That was all the energy he could muster, and I was glad he got to watch, even though I thought he really wanted to throw some darts himself. He was an excellent player.

We were still having our breakfast dates. It was just our thing, and we enjoyed it. When he shared pictures of flying drones or eating out or having a walk, there were comments like, "You don't look sick, are you sure you're at end stage?"

Those to him were mean. I guessed when he was given the prognosis to his life, he wanted to live it to the maximum. I guessed when he knew the time will come when he couldn't go out, he wanted to go out as much as he could. I guessed when he knew he'd be leaving his wife, he wanted to take her out as often as he could. He was sad with such comments. But he never said it out loud to others. He didn't want to offend people when they were ones offending him. That was him. He swallowed so many comments which people thought were harmless yet said nothing of it. He only confided in me on the disappointments. Like when some asked if they've tried this remedy or tried that remedy, instead of asking how his new hobby was. Like when people said he shouldn't trust the doctor but to trust only Allah. He trusted Allah's will, but he also thought there was a need to prepare and create memories for the people he was leaving. He was annoyed when people contacted him and only wanted to talk about the dreadful disease. He felt it was as if that was all anyone was interested with.

"I am more than just my cancer," he sighed. "Everyone just wants to ask about the cancer."

At home, we rarely bring up this cancer issue. We talked like any normal family would. We yelled at our kids like any barely sane parents of large families would. We did chores, and we planned for weekend. We had routines that kept us busy. We argued, we made up, and we made time.

FOURTEEN

Hospice Care

When the doctor at the cancer centre told us that no more treatment will be arranged, we were referred to receive hospice care at home. This was something new to me, and it became a relationship like no other, us and HCA.

HCA's services started almost immediately. The nurse who was to be taking my Warrior's case came with a team doctor to assess the situation and then let us in on what their services entailed. They were there to prepare us. They explained what could happen before the end. It was also their job to handle pain management and to titrate my Warrior's medication. My Warrior was, at that point, on morphine to control the pain. Over the course, more pain management medication came into play.

At first, I wasn't comfortable and felt like it was rather insensitive. After all, my Warrior was still standing tall that September 2021. Nothing about him screamed terminally ill. To be honest, I wasn't prepared to listen.

Not only nursing care aspects were explained to us, but we also had a social worker. His role was to check on how we were emotionally, socially, and financially. He thought us how to tap on the Warrior's funds at the CPF to tide things over, to do the things he liked, and to settle on financial obligations, such as debts or backdated bills. He also checked on the children's well-being.

The hospice care team came for a visit every fortnight at first. Towards the end of my Warrior's life, the nurse came every week.

Hospice care team was also the team who would eventually help us with the rental of hospital bed, commode, oxygen concentrator. They were also the one who sent a child therapist, a trainer to get me up to speed on how to care when my Warrior entered bedridden stage. And they were also the ones to provide samples and ideas. It was like having a mentor and a cheerleader.

So no matter how much they were telling me the gory details, they were the ones who provided the correct help in each step.

FIFTEEN

#theselamatsgoumrah

"I've spoken to Hakeem, and he's going to arrange for us to go for Umrah."

It was November 2021. Hakeem was his nephew and ran a successful funeral service and had experience in managing groups for Umrah.

"Next year?" I asked.

"No, Dinda . . . December. This December 2021." He smiled.

Umrah – the small non-mandatory pilgrimage made by Muslims to Mecca, Saudi Arabia, which may be performed at any time of the year. Usually, the package would include a couple of days in Madinah, Saudi Arabia, as well.

"What's the rush, Abang?" I asked, flipping the calendar, completely not remembering that my Warrior had that prognosis.

He said, "I want to go. I've always wanted to take you. You've always wanted to go. If I don't take you now, no one else will."

I choked. He remembered my dream and that I had said if we ever have the means, I want us to go there. I wanted to turn on the floodgates when he said if he didn't take me, no one else will. It was just so foretelling.

That was my Warrior, he who strived to make all my dreams, needs, and wants come true. When I said I wanted to wear purple for our wedding, he replied with "Let's do it!" When I was looking at a pink watch at the shop and thought it was too expensive, he saved and surprised me with it. When I had a craving for the silliest of food, he picked up the car keys and said, "Go get ready." Or he's get them for me and brought them home with a grin on his face. "I know you love me," he'd say with a silly grin on his face. "I love you too."

I remembered he didn't know what the craze with bubble tea was and had no idea what the flavours were. Yet he went and got me one, picked me up from the office with bubble tea next to my seat.

If he made extra from driving, he spent it on me or the kids, little things he picked up from the petrol station, a stopover at the *kuih* shop, or something he ordered online to benefit us. If we're planning to go out on Sunday, he worked doubly hard on Saturday so he has enough to cover his expenditure and something to spoil us. He beamed with pride when he could afford to buy a gold bracelet. "You deserve everything, Dinda."

Once he got my family and best friend in on a surprise for my birthday. He booked the Ritz Carlton Millenia Hotel for an overnight stay and told them to hide in the room to surprise me. I might have mentioned once or twice about what it would be like to have a staycation there. He remembered it and made it a reality. We were in a suite, and I never asked how he was paying for that stay.

I asked if we have the budget for the Umrah journey, seeing that we were doing some works on the house. After ten years of living in the house, we could finally do the kitchen, change the doors and window grills. When we moved in, we didn't have much and had just reused what the past owner had left. We only did the two bathrooms for hygiene reasons and painted the house so it looked fresh. My Warrior wanted to give me the house I deserved and started to engage people to start working.

"Don't worry, we do. And you can get whatever you need to have a good trip. But can you handle the communication after this? I don't think I can."

So with just above a month to be ready, I scuttled with all the preparations, buying things for the trip, making payments, making appointments for vaccinations, passport renewals, and one very important thing: getting his oncologist and hospice doctor convinced that my Warrior was fit for the trip. That would mean I have to make sure he was somewhat stable and healthy enough to fly and be away from the familiar medical facility. Not much convincing was needed. My Warrior was in such high spirits that he was feeling fine most of the time.

The oncologist and hospice team issued the letter for flight. The team also helped ensure we have all the medication he would need and also standby.

We also needed to be spiritually prepared. I was nervous and excited. We have not travelled for so long! And we're going to the utmost place that every Muslim would want to be. And I'm going with my Warrior! We watched YouTube clips, went for the one-day briefing his nephew did, and read a lot. My Warrior did not seem as excited as I am. In fact, he was subdued most of the time. I soon realised he was worried that he may not make it there, given the prognosis that was given to him. Of course, everything was Allah's will. But he didn't want to get too excited. He finally showed some excitement a day before we left. When he knew that he was well enough and had also cleared the Covid test for travelling.

My parents stayed over to take care of the kids whilst we were away for thirteen days. The kitchen was still on renovation, with our countertops being installed the day we left.

The day we flew was the last time my Warrior could carry a bag on his shoulders. After that, his strength just started depleting. It was also the last time that he had the full function of his legs.

The flight was above eight hours, and my Warrior developed water retention on his legs. His left leg, especially, was really swollen, and it made him have difficulty to walk. But determination superseded that.

SIXTEEN

Madinah Sky

The first road trip was from Jeddah to Madinah, right after we touched down. We managed to sleep through the journey, but by then, my Warrior was extremely exhausted. He kept really quiet as he didn't want to worry the group. There were sixteen of us, family on his side. His right rib was in pain as well. When we reached Madinah, just a few minutes before *Subuh* prayer, we went all quiet at the glimpses of Masjid Nabawi, the Prophet's mosque. I couldn't believe we were finally here and that our hotel was just across the street!

The Warrior was not up for it to have his first prayer at the mosque, tired out with all the travelling and in pain. He needed to be in the comforts of bed immediately. We did our *Subuh* in our room, and I unpacked whilst taking care of him whilst he rested. We prayed that he would be well enough for the afternoon as it would be Friday prayers. Friday prayers at Masjid Nabawi was too great to be missed.

And he mustered all his strength to attend. I was so proud of him! He even made it to the rooftop of the mosque to be with the men of the group. He wasn't going to miss the chance. He told me stories of the view from up there later on in the day. He told it with such happiness. I was so happy to watch him.

The rest of the time we were in Madinah was filled with ups and downs. By the second day we were there, his nephew, who was in charge of our group, had to arrange for wheelchair. The water retention and pain on rib were making it difficult for him to walk, and he was uncomfortable. The cooler air was also not making it easy on his breathing. But he was still in high spirits, a little quieter than usual, but he's in good mood most of the time. He rested a lot, having meals in our room. *Maghrib* and *Isyak* were prayer times that we will go to the mosque together because he remembered that I wanted to watch the sky turned purple and pink at close to *Maghrib* and all throughout *Maghrib*. Madinah has gorgeous purple-pink hues in the sky, in the early morning as the sun rises and evening as the sun sets. And it was my dream to pray under that sky. So he made it a point to try to be go to Masjid Nabawi with me on those times. He braved the cold of 12 degrees Celsius and blowing wind in the morning and entertained my happiness of praying in the open as the sun sets. Like how often can one pray in the open air in the coolness of the evening?

I'd push him in the wheelchair, walked through the gates, and somehow will more than always takeover to push him to the men's prayer area whilst I make my way to the women's area. Strangers were willing to lend that helping hand. Sometimes the kind cleaners would help. He made friends with one of them and exchanged numbers. My Warrior was in communication through WhatsApp with the kind man even after we returned home. Once the prayer is done and we've had our personal time with our *doa* and *zikir*, my Warrior would wait patiently for me at the women's entrance. He was always there before me. He didn't want me to be lost.

"I'll always wait for you, okay? You don't worry."

This man was in a wheelchair, and yet he never felt that he should let go of his responsibility to take care of his wife, especially in a foreign land. My eyes would always look for him in a crowd. Once, I went for *Asar* prayers on my own whilst he rested in our room. I went out of the prayer area and was almost frantically looking for him, only to remember that he didn't come along. I told him this hilarious story when I went back to our room, and he smiled.

And he went with me for every prayer in the mosque from then on and expected me to stay with him to pray in the room when he couldn't. But he still made sure we went for *Subuh*, *Maghrib*, and *Isyak* to the mosque because he knew how important it was to me.

And just like in the Maldives, where we walked head up looking at the blanket of stars in the sky, we walked staring up at the pink and purple sky. It was the most magical time.

My Warrior participated in the itinerary, even with his condition. I had to make sure that he had his pain medication on time, diet was taken care of, and rest was enough. The visit to Raudhah-ul-Jannah (Garden of Paradise) was one that he most anticipated. The women and men have separate entrances; hence, he went with the men in our group. His other nephew pushed him on the wheelchair. Later that night, he told me that he got to pray at the front and for a very long time. He cried and cried. I wanted to ask what he prayed for but thought it was between him and Allah. He never asked what I prayed for either.

But he said, "I also prayed that whatever you prayed for will come true. If it doesn't, trust in Allah. The best is already planned for you."

I stared at him sleeping that night. There was peace in his expression, almost as if there was no pain. I snuggled to him gently. I couldn't sleep. I had a short visit on the outside of Jannat Al Baqi, peeping in. It was the utmost graveyard that Muslims would just love to be buried there. I stared long and hard through the barriers. Death is a promise. We just don't know when and how.

I hardly sleep whilst we were in Madinah. I felt that it was my duty to make sure he was all right, to make sure I prepare everything, to be fully awake when he needed pain medication, to rub ointment on his back and rib, to ensure his legs were raised nicely whilst sleeping so the water retention could be helped, to make sure I was on hand (and feet) when he needed to use the bathroom.

We visited the Prophet's grave area, Masjid Quba, Jabal Uhud, Jabal Rummat, Dar Al Madinah Museum, and a dates plantation with the group. On our own, we went on night walks every night after dinner. *Maghrib* and *Isyak* are really close in timing there. Hence, once we're done with dinner, after completing prayers, it was night walks for us. Just exploring the area around our hotel, sitting outside Masjid Nabawi to enjoy the atmosphere, getting coffee, a little bit of shopping, taking photographs, and just enjoying our time together. I'd push him all around. He would ask if I was tired, but I was never tired. I lived for moments.

On our final evening in Madinah, we were happy to have the experience but was utterly sad to leave the city. Our night walk was long. We even walked a bit more during the day.

"Let's come here again, Abang. I just love it here. Can we stay here longer the next time we're here? We come during this kind of weather again, ya? I just love the cold."

My Warrior smiled at my absolute glee. "Insya Allah, Dinda." God willing. "You sure you want to come and push me around again?" he asked, still smiling.

"In a heartbeat." I smiled back and hugged him.

I'd never have that ever again.

SEVENTEEN

Mood in Makkah

Clad in our best whites, we set out for Holy Makkah. Our first Umrah was to be carried out after we checked into the hotel and had dinner.

We bade farewell to Rasulullah after *Subuh* prayer, watched the famous umbrellas open up. It was our last pink and purple sky, and I cried. We took a walk along the mosque complex before making our way for breakfast. My Warrior laughed that I was having falafels for every breakfast time and never got bored. Those were not the only things I ate, but he made it sound like I was falafel crazy.

"Do you want to pack some for our journey to Makkah, Dinda?" he joked.

The act of Umrah is to perform *Tawaf* of the *Kaabah* and *Sa'ee* between the hills of Safa and Marwah, after assuming the state of *Ihram* from a Meeqat.

The moment my Warrior dressed in his *Ihram*, I felt a tinge of happiness and sadness; happy that he was finally about to get what he wished for, sad that this all white is what we would all be when our time on earth is up. I remembered my Warrior beaming at me when I got into my white *jubah* and white hijab.

"Beautiful, lah, my wife," he said.

My Warrior rested for the entire journey to Makkah. He needed to conserve the energy as it was going to be a long day and a long night.

His nephew had arranged for someone to assist in pushing my Warrior through the act of Umrah. I was to perform mine with the group. This is so we have that peace of mind that our Umrah will be performed correctly. I didn't like the separation. I was worried for his safety. What if something happened midway? I didn't like being away from him. But I understood that it was necessary and concentrated on my own act.

That feeling when I saw the *Kaabah* for the very first time in front of my eyes was simply mesmerising, a sense of awakening. I wished I could share that moment with my Warrior, but I guessed that would make for a story when I meet him at the hotel room later. The prayers that followed after the *Tawaf* were begging, tearful, heartfelt, and emotionally draining. There were a lot of people around me, but it felt like I was crying on my own.

I met my Warrior back at the hotel, all clean shaven to complete his act. He was tired, but there was a glow about him I couldn't quite describe. There was just that light on his face. We exchanged stories of our experience. We slept really late that night as we talked and laughed.

Whilst my Warrior was not feeling too great in Madinah, he was a lot better in Makkah. He went for prayers at the mosque more often, walking from our hotel to the Masjidil Haram. The wheelchair was only used to go around the area, visits, perform the acts of Umrah, perform additional acts of *Tawaf*, and shop. For prayers calls, we walked. We'd leave our hotel room much earlier than others and walked slowly to Masjidil Haram. This time I waited at the compounds for him to come out, my eyes scanning a sea of people for that one who has my heart. We managed to spot each other all the time. He always had a smile once he spotted me. And I always felt the butterflies. Paris is not a city of love, Makkah is.

My Warrior was such in wonderful mood, and his strength seemed to heighten whilst we were in Makkah. We visited Jabal Thur, Jabal Rahmah. The air was definitely different here as we felt like newlyweds. We saw a *kiswah* production, went to a museum, and of course, had lots of date nights. New York is not the city that never sleeps, Makkah is, especially after *Isyak* when it was just bustling. We went for walks, snacks, shopping for fragrances and precious stones, and also to the hyper-mart, twice. Imagine a full hyper-mart with all things *halal*. Our luggage was filled with snacks.

A trip to the Taif area was exceptional. It was so cold up in the highlands. We went to a rose garden, Masjid Abdullah bin Abbas, ate authentic nasi mandi, and had fresh fruits and tea in foggy weather.

"Can you imagine that I took you to Europe?" he asked.

"This is better than Europe," I answered.

He smiled. The cold was torturous for him, but he powered on. He loved seeing me enjoying the cold.

My Warrior ate well, slept well, and was generally well. There were finally photos of him standing next to me instead of sitting in a wheelchair all the time. He was cracking jokes, being his friendly self, snacking around, and was in high spirits.

Because he was in a wheelchair for the act of Umrah, he got the opportunity to be close to the *Kaabah*, seeing the Hajar Aswad closer. I was on the outer circle. My Warrior wanted so bad to let me have that experience. So we did *Tawaf Sunat* on one of the nights, seven rounds of surrealness around the *Kaabah*.

"I've always wanted to bring you here, Dinda. And now it is fulfilled," he said as we left the circle.

My prayers were, again, tearful. I sat behind him and watched him pray, begged Allah, and literally broke down. He had gotten out of the wheelchair and sat on the pristine and cold white marble floor. It seemed that his prayers were never ending. And then he stopped and sat there staring at the *Kaabah* for a while, buried his face in his palms, and shook his head. He turned around to me and said the same thing he said in Madinah, "I also prayed that whatever you prayed for will come true. If it doesn't, trust in Allah. The best is already planned for you." And he added, "I love you, and thank you for being my wife. No matter what happens next, it's you and me."

Tears never left me.

We did another act of Umrah and another set of *Tawaf* before we left Makkah, four times on the white floors, four times drenched with tears.

He never told me what he prayed for. I never told him what I prayed for. But I take into comfort that we had prayed for the same things because no matter what happened, it'll always be my Warrior and me.

Although it was emotional, being in Makkah, we managed to squeeze in some fun. We felt that we needed to make the most of our moments there. We had each other, and that was what mattered. He bought me a gorgeous white abaya, for Hari Raya, he said. Well then, I guessed we were going to wear white for Hari Raya.

On the final might in Makkah, we went on an extended night walk. We bade farewell to a shopkeeper with whom we had made friends. We stood in the outer compounds of Masjidil Haram and soaked in the atmosphere.

We bought a walking stick. We figured my Warrior would need one now. He was in the wheelchair most of the time whilst we were in the Middle East, and his legs were not really healthily functioning. Walking stick-shopping in Makkah was fun. There were so many choices, from super simple to super fancy. We found one at a mall in our hotel, tried on a few for fit, and finally, we found one that my Warrior liked. He used the walking stick a lot when we came home.

In the morning, before we left Makkah, we did *Tawaf Wada*, a farewell to the holiest land. I pushed him in the wheelchair. I did as slowly as I could. As the seventh round approached, I shed a tear.

We prayed with the rest of the group. Not one was dry-eyed as we said our thank you and apologised for any mistakes we may have done.

Last, I hugged my Warrior and said my sorry and thanked him for being here with me. I told him I hoped all his prayers will come true. I told him he was the best husband one can ever pray for.

He cried and said his thanks and sorry. He prayed only the best for me. And the best line for a wife, "I *redha* with you as my wife."

I cried. "We need to come here again, Abang." I said in between sobs.

He said, "Insya Allah, Dinda." Allah's will.

We never will.

Our flight back to Singapore was at night. With hours to spare, we were brought to a mall near the airport. So we freshened up and shopped a little. My Warrior and I went to a chocolate café for date. We had crepes and tea whilst talking about the entire trip. Again, we felt like newlyweds. Throughout that trip, there was nothing that I wanted to do or get that my Warrior had said no to. Apart from fulfilling religious obligations successfully, he wanted me to have great time. It was "Anything you want, Dinda."

It was to be our very last trip together.

EIGHTEEN

Slide

When we were waiting to board the plane home from Jeddah, my Warrior wasn't in a very good shape. He was tired, in pain, and needed to lie down. Being in a wheelchair for hours isn't comfortable. And as with airports, the hassle just dragged. I remembered whispering into his ears, "Please, Abang, hang in there a little bit more, at least 'til we get you nicely settled in the aircraft. We want to go back to Singapore, ya."

I didn't want us to be stuck in a foreign hospital so close to flying home. The trip was over, and I want us to be on familiar grounds if he needed the medical attention. But I knew he was simply very tired and needed to rest. I prayed for a smooth boarding.

The airline transported him right into the cabin and offered us a whole of seats to ourselves. My Warrior and I could lie down to sleep throughout the flight home! There was also no one else close to us, so there was a bit of privacy. I gave my Warrior his pain medication, and he went to sleep almost as soon as we got into the sky. I was relieved. I woke him up for meals, which he diligently ate, bread rolls and all. I chatted with him in between. He was starting to be himself again after a few hours of rest. Thank Allah.

I stared out of the window into the dark sky, tears rolling down my face. This trip was over, a heavy weight in my heart. As we landed, I sat next to my Warrior and let him squeeze my hand. He knew I get edgy at take-off and landing. He would usually have his hands engulfing mine to calm me. That one felt different. It felt more comforting than before. It felt unusually strong.

"It's okay, Dinda. I got you." And he squeezed even harder.

Disembarking was him being strapped to a wheelchair, assisted by the airport staff all the way through immigration and Covid test area, and then finally, at the gates. Our great friend, Shahri, was already waiting for us. He had sent us off and then drove our twins to school and back whilst we were away. I was so anxious to get home to see the children again. But I also had a sinking feeling as I glanced out of the car window, an overwhelming sadness. My Warrior was chatting happily with Shahri. I was glad he was even talking that much.

The children were all home when we reached. They were all excited to check what he had in our luggage. My Warrior entertained them for a while, joking and laughing. He told them some stories. An hour later, he showered and went for a long nap.

We were on home quarantine for the next seven days as a Covid precaution. My Warrior never went back to work after that. He could no longer drive long hours. His driving became to send the children to school and to fetch them home, to go grocery-shopping with me, to go for breakfast dates with me, to bring the family out once in a while, to get new plants with me.

His health was beginning to slide. The pain on his upper back and rib was keeping him up at night and very uncomfortable during the day. Sometimes ointment and pain medication worked. Other times it got so excruciating that I felt helpless. We knew this was going to happen.

Despite that, we managed to plan a staycation with the children as we stepped into 2022. We booked a one-night stay at Hyatt, two connecting suites to fit the seven of us. We stayed indoors. The boys, Arfan and Eshan, and I went out to get dinner and treats. Sarah and the twins stayed with their Papa in the room whilst doing craftwork. Later at night, we played Jenga and Uno. My Warrior joined us for a couple of games. But he was the first one heading to bed. Hotel bed, as comfortable as it was, was not his bed. And he didn't really sleep well. We all went for a buffet breakfast, took some pictures, and headed back to our room. The children had their bathtub play time, more rounds of Jenga, and just handing out. I packed whilst my Warrior napped. It used to be a tag team: I would pack, and my Warrior would attend to the children. I would hear him laugh and kid around with the children, just plainly being silly. Now the children were on their own and disengaged from him, whilst he could only lie down to rest. I knew he was miserable inside. He was, after all, very involved in his children's daily life.

He tried within his means to be involved with the children's first day of the school year. He could still drive, and he was proud that he could still do that. He said that was the least he could do for the children.

He felt like he wasn't doing much for them and that I was the one running around a lot. I thought, as long as he was involved in something, no matter how small, I was sure the children would appreciate. They were all aware of his situation, and I've told them that their Papa's health was deteriorating. If anything, I thought they've been very forgiving and understanding towards his condition, far beyond what we could ask for.

The months of January and February is our cake season. Eshan and the twins' birthdays were in January. Arfan, Sarah, and my birthdays were in February. So during these two months, we had cakes almost every other week. Birthdays are always celebrated in this house. And this year, we did just that—cake, treats, presents, and everything. We did it as usual. But sometimes the usual are the ones that holds the most memories. My Warrior was the kind of father who will make time for his children's birthdays. When he was out driving, he would ask me what time he needed to be home for the celebration. And he'll be back at least an hour before with extra treats in his hands. He would try as much as he could to get what we wanted for our birthdays. He loved birthdays because he didn't have as much fun of a celebration and wanted our children to have what he never had. His birthday was in August. The only one in our family with a birthday further down the year. And we have always made it extra special for the man of our house.

I'm glad that we had made birthdays a big deal. As much as we wanted to create memories for the children, they were also moments for us to reflect and reminisce. We remember the time our children were born, and we made sure we made everyone feel special.

We went for a routine check-up at the cancer centre, and the water retention issue on my Warrior's legs was an issue that prompted an ultrasound to rule out any blood clots. There was none; all praise to Allah.

We also scheduled one radiation treatment to ease the pain on bis right rib. It was only one shot this time, but I couldn't make it as the timing clashed with Sarah and Eshan's school dismissal. His friend, Shahri, accompanied him. Just one session but radiation created havoc in his system, his mind, and his strength. The children watched as he crashed at the sofa. They have watched their Papa through so many episodes, and they didn't have anyone to confide to but one another. It wasn't easy for them to go through the motions of their Papa's mood swings. Pain really did evil to the mind. One moment he'd be crying, another moment vicious anger, and the next moment agitated.

When my Warrior felt up to it, he'll still go out to fly his drones. I tagged along with my laptop. I have been fortunate enough that my employers were aware of what was going on and were supportive. I had been very frank and truthful with them. I had told my boss everything as it went along. I had even called her when my Warrior was admitted to the hospital.

One afternoon the morphine and fentanyl patch were just failing my Warrior. He was in constant pain, and nothing seemed to work. He was yelling and groaning in severe pain. In the end, he told me to call for the ambulance and take him to the hospital. I packed his necessities, made a few phone calls, and left Sarah and Eshan at home to wait for my mother, whilst I went with my Warrior to Sengkang General Hospital. There, all they could do was to administer the same form of pain medication, wait, and see. There was pretty much nothing they could do for terminal stages of cancer. With the Covid restrictions, I was only allowed very short visits. I brought him clean clothes, his favourite butter cookies, and *bidara* ointment to rub on his back to relax some of the pain. I applied some ointment on his back before I left the hospital, just to make him feel better. He stayed for two nights. On the third night, he called me and asked me to pick him up. He had asked to be released. He realised there was nothing anyone could do for him. I picked him up, and we went home. He seemed to know that from then on, pain will need to be managed as is.

I was shaken with this episode. It was scary. Because you have that prognosis of less than a year lingering around, this emergency shook me to the core, like it could happen. It really could happen. What if it really happened and that was it? I was so scared. I slept with my hand in his, buried my face in his arms a couple of times that night. I was losing him, and that thought saddened me, ripped my heart. He felt that, touched my face and wiped my tears.

"You'll be okay, Dinda. I'm here." For how long? A question I didn't dare to even ask.

Two days later, he could drive again. Normalcy set in, with him driving to send the children to school, and he rested a lot in between. I decided to take leave from work to spend some time with him. Breakfast date, of course. We went to a bookshop, a plant nursery, walked about in Geylang Serai, and talked in the car as we always did. My Warrior even walked without his walking stick. We walked holding hands, smiling. It was as if that scary episode never happened. We picked up the children when it was time to.

Over the next few weeks, I made time for more breakfast dates before I started my work for the day. I worked at home; hence, we were together 24/7. We'd send the children to school, head for our breakfast date, and make our way home in time for me to turn on the laptop and get my work done. After that hospital scare, he had wanted me to work by his side. So I would just set up my laptop wherever he was resting.

That hospitalisation episode also prompted the hospice team to request for a procedure to be done on my Warrior's rib to block a nerve to subside the pain. The procedure was an injection, and it was done promptly.

It worked for a while, but the pain came back about a month after. Pain medication was then titrated, adjusted by the pain management team at Sengkang General Hospital and the hospice team. That was the last procedure to ever be done on my Warrior's body.

March came, and it was a school break. We planned another one-night staycation, this time at Goodwood Hotel. We booked two connecting rooms, but they gave us the huge Mayfair Suite! The children were ecstatic as the room was huge, with dining area and overlooking the pool downstairs. We had pool time! My Warrior didn't dip in with the us, but he did come down and joined us poolside, which made the children really happy because their Papa joined their activity. My Warrior wasn't feeling very well in the hotel room and preferred to lie down most of the time. He didn't really join us at games or chitchat. He only joined us for meals. We let the children have the huge bed. I slept on the floor, next to his single bed. I was worried for him and wanted to be within inches from him in case he needed to go to the bathroom or needed help in the middle of the night. I was worried he would fall. As usual, we took our customary family pictures for memories, memories that we now hold dearly.

My Warrior was extremely tired when we came home. He slept for the remainder of the day. A few moments later, he was up to his normal self again. But we noticed that the right side of his face was drooping. His facial nerves had taken a toll. Over time it impacted his ability to chew and to close his right eye. At first, we thought it was like when I had Bell's Palsy. But it turned out, it was a sign of deterioration. His body was rapidly sending signals of decline.

He was driving lesser and lesser. On many days, I was sending the children to school by taking the bus. He just could not get himself up in the morning. Sometimes he'd be fine midday, just in time to join me to picking Sarah and Eshan from school. Sometimes he'd be okay to come along to pick up Naela and Nadra at preschool. Sometimes none, I'd be doing them all.

Nights were also pretty difficult. My Warrior got restless, unable to sleep well. He'd be talking in his sleep or deciding to walk around the house all of a sudden. I'd be up, accompanying him. I didn't want him to be on his own. There were times that he'd be in pain, and the painkillers were not taking effect quick enough. He suffered and I would feel so helpless. But I knew I had to do anything I could to be his number one cheerleader. I would always try to put him at ease or be with him with a smile on my face so he would not worry about disturbing me. How could he be disturbing me? I was tired, of course. But he was never a burden to me. And I made sure I told him this all the time. If I'm not smiling, it was only because I am a human, and I get tired. But I love him very much and he was never a burden in any way. I told him this repeatedly, even on the night before he passed on.

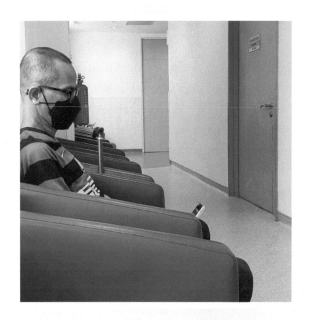

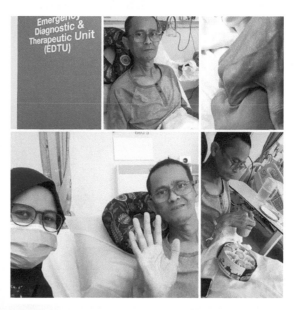

NINETEEN

The Last Ramadan and Aidilfitri

Ramadan is the ninth month of the Islamic calendar. We observe this with a month of fasting, prayer, reflection, and giving back to the community.

My Warrior loved Ramadan for various reasons. It's a month of prayers, where good deeds are rewarded in folds and the simplest act of kindness yields a field of greatness. Who didn't like that? So he would strive as much as he could to do more than usual. Unfortunately, in 2022, he couldn't fast as he needed to take his medication on time and more frequently. He also needed to keep his water intake in check, and he had to eat, albeit small meals. He was very sad, to say the least. He really wanted to fast. Since he couldn't, he decided to do more donations to the needy, helped me prepare food for breaking fast, and prayed a lot more.

But the one thing he avoided was waking up for Sahur with us. *Sahur* is the meal eaten before dawn during Ramadan, after which Muslims will fast until after sunset. Usually, he would keep up with me whilst I prepare the food before walking up Arfan, Sarah, and Eshan. He would giggle at Eshan's antics and Sarah's dishevelled hair. This year, however, he just slept through. Even though he wasn't going to fast, I was hoping he would accompany the children. But he just ignored us. I thought he was feeling ashamed in front of the children. After all, he always told them to try as hard as they could to fast during Ramadan, and yet he was the one who had to skip. Now I think he was actually starting to create a distance with the children.

We managed to bring the children to bazaars and prepare for Hari Raya. We usually wear matching outfits at least for first day of Hari Raya. This year we were wearing white. I've mine that my Warrior chose for me in Makkah. He was going to wear the white *jubah* he got before our Umrah trip. It was his favourite.

So I ordered the children's white/cream outfits. A little foretelling, their outfits became the white outfits they wore the day we sent our Warrior to his forever home.

My Warrior didn't join us for predawn meals, but he joined us when it was time to break the fast. In fact, he looked forward to that because he was spoiling us with the things we loved to eat. He'd ask us what we'd like to have to the day and tried his best to go out and get them. I, of course, have to tag along as he continued his quest to hunt for the things his children would like to see on the table at 7:00 p.m.

That was my Warrior. Whatever the children wanted to eat, he will try to get them because he loved seeing their faces lighting up and enjoying the food. Like when Naela had a liking for *Kunafe* and *Kadaif*, he got them for her several times because he was so happy that she liked what he was also fond of. And Naela had an eating style that he loved to stare at and laugh. He was always buying durian for Eshan because that boy absolutely loves durians. Eshan takes after him so much, especially in food favourites. He would grab a pack of gummies or surprise eggs for the girls when he was at the petrol station. And it was not just the children, for me as well. He was that thoughtful father and husband, who has his family filling his heart.

Hari Raya preparation also meant decorating the house. My Warrior was going all out! We got new serving plates, carpets, and whatever decorations he wanted. He would have called the curtains people if I didn't tell him to take step back. It would be rather costly. He seemed to want his family to have everything this Hari Raya, no holds barred.

Hari Raya Aidilfitri arrived. My Warrior was extremely happy. He smiled a lot whilst getting ready. We had the festive meal, which I had made sure nothing was spicy. My Warrior could no longer eat anything spicy at that point. It was sad as he loved spicy food. *Asam Pedas*, curries, *lemak Cili Padi*, *Sambal Belacan*, and *Sambal Tumis* were all up his alley. He was my spicy food buddy. I made his favourite *Ayam Masak Hijau* and *Rendang* non-spicy. He ate them all, in small portions, but he ate them. Apart from no longer being able to consume spicy food, not even a tinge of chilli, my Warrior's food portion was as small as the twins', sometimes even smaller. But I was just happy that he was eating and snacking. Whenever he loved a certain kind of biscuits, I made sure I stocked them up. And I'll accompany him whilst he snacked. I was not worried if he didn't finish his lunch or dinner as long as he ate. There were people telling me what I should feed him and what he shouldn't be eating. I would smile and nod. I have seen him not being able to swallow anything during radiation and a little more after. I have seen him eyed at food, not being able to have a bite. I have seen how he loved his food and how he loved his medium steak. So when he wanted to eat now, whatever he wanted now, I gave him. And I no longer wanted to force him to eat anything he didn't want. I didn't have the heart to enforce anything. That was my husband, I couldn't deprive him of the things he loved and enforce the things he didn't.

We welcomed guests into our home and even went visiting to a couple of houses through the month of Aidilfitri whenever my Warrior was feeling up for it. He'll walk with his walking stick, slowly making steps. His steps, I noticed, got even slower that month. It was May 2022. He got tired more easily. His sleep was less peaceful. He would be talking or groaning in his sleep. Sometimes he would wake up and walked around. I'd also get up when he's up, worried that he might fall or get emotional. I wanted him to know I'm always with him.

The final week of Aidilfitri was when things took into a sharper decline. On 23 May, we had guests over and then went out to visit two families, a normal Hari Raya affair. That night my Warrior crashed, too tired to even speak. When we woke up the next day, he said he needed to sleep in. So I got the children ready for school and sent them all. That day my Warrior was so tired that he slept the entire day. On 25 May, we said goodbye to the car. My Warrior could no longer walk more than a couple of steps around the house. He finally said he could no longer drive. Shahri made the necessary arrangement with the car.

That day was a hard day. I wished I could have one more spin with my Warrior in the driver's seat. But that wasn't possible as he could no longer drive. Was I sad? Of course, I was, not the selfish kind but because of a time lost.

Why Ezmien didn't have a license? Because she was never made to feel she needed one since she met her Warrior. He ferried her to wherever she needed/wanted to go, short ones to get coffee or long ones into Malaysia. She asked, and he lovingly drove. He ferried her to work and waited promptly when she finished every day. He even met her for lunch and drove to wherever she wanted to eat. She remembered late night Johor Bahru trips. She remembered the drive home after their Masjid Sultan solemnisation. She remembered *balik kampong* trips. She remembered drives to Kuala Lumpur. She remembered grocery runs. She remembered coming home after the births of their children. She remembered snacking in the car. She remembered the school runs. She remembered stuffing the car with Ikea buys and plant-shopping. She remembered all the dates they squeezed in between. She even remembered all the misbehaving the kids have done in the car. She remembered all the rides for breakfast dates and late-night coffee.

"Why Ezmien didn't have a license?"

Because she's been treated like the queen, his queen.

I was devastated as I knew this will never be repeated. A time has passed. I wasn't the only one who felt a loss.

Coming out from the mosque one Saturday after her religious class, Sarah's eyes scanned the many cars parked on the service road, the same way Nadra was a few days back when she came out from the childcare centre. I knew they missed being picked up by their Papa, who never failed to be there, rain or shine. Sarah, until recently, never really needed to always be taking the bus or even be walking to the bus stop. She's been ferried for nine years of her life.

"Will Papa walk again, Mom?" One syllable to my name means she was being serious. "Mommy" was for when they *manja* or wanted something.

A part of me wanted to say yes and remain hopeful. After all, Allah's will. A more realistic part of me said, "No," instead.

"But he's using your walking thing now, and you walked again," my walking aid from when I was recovering from a road accident.

I decided to just keep walking to the bus stop and distracted her with another conversation. I let her choose whatever she wanted from the shop opposite where we live.

There were things that popped out of the children's mouth that I struggle to find the correct answer to. It was a myth that moms had answers to everything.

Nadra had more than once asked, "When will Papa drive again?" I missed being ferried too.

Raya dragged for a few more days, and my Warrior continued his decline. We finally called the hospice care to let them know we now needed the hospital bed to be installed. It came the day after. The HCA team was extremely dependable. Whenever I needed something, they had it on standby.

I rearranged the living area so we can have the hospital bed installed near the living room window. That way, he was still at the centre of our attention, still within our everyday activities. The window overlooked his plants at the corridor, and he could see the children going out and coming home. He got the sun, and he could see when night came. The TV was also in front of him so he won't get bored. I was working by his bedside and could see him from the kitchen when I'm cooking. He was never out of my sight when I'm doing house chores. I was at his beck and call at any time. I could watch his favourite dramas and TV shows with him whilst working through my cases or replying to e-mails. I'm just a few steps away when he needed to go to the bathroom. I'd help him sit up to have his drinks, meals, and medication; helped him lie down when he needed to rest; got him his milk, juice, or whatever he felt like having.

News travelled fast of his declining condition, and everyone wanted to visit. Guests streamed in almost daily from then on, various groups, not just extended family. My Warrior was a very friendly man. We had guests who were his former schoolmates and former neighbours, from national services buddies to school bandmates, from first job to last job, and everyone else he knew in between. We had guests calling to come and those who just popped up. We had guests bringing dinner and guests bringing blessings. We had guests coming over to keep it light with laughter and old stories and guests who cried out in the open. It was a daily affair! We were exhausted but also happy to see that my Warrior made that kind of impact on others that they came all the way to visit him. He was a great man. And I was so glad he saw that.

TWENTY
Tenth

We loved our wedding anniversary and would always look forward to the date because we couldn't believe that we were given a second chance to build a lifetime of love—our love story. Second marriages for us meant we worked a lot more to make it work. We didn't want it to fail.

We celebrated every anniversary. We went to Bali for one. That was incredible. Our flight home was right at the midnight of the actual date. My Warrior said, "Happy anniversary, Dinda, an anniversary in the sky. You always loved looking at the sky." We held hands the entire flight.

The month of May was not only Hari Raya Aidilfitri that year, but it was also our tenth anniversary and Mother's Day. On one of our shopping trips to get ready for Hari Raya, my Warrior told me to push his wheelchair to a jewellery shop. Yes, in May, my Warrior needed to go around in the wheelchair sometimes, when his legs were too weak and when he didn't want to exert his ribs. He told me to pick a bracelet, one that I would never buy on my own. It was to be my tenth anniversary gift as well as for Mother's Day. My Warrior was no longer able to surprise me and wanted me to pick what I would love.

"Are you sure?" I asked.

"Yes, anything you want. You're my great love and mother to my children. Anniversary and Mother's Day is all for you."

I picked, whilst hiding my tears, a classic piece. I wore it all through Hari Raya, and he beamed every time.

On the day of our anniversary, we had a breakfast picnic planned. At that time, on 11 May 2022, my Warrior could still drive. We were to send the children to school and then head over to get breakfast packed and head over to the beach for a date. And he would be flying his drone. But on that morning, he couldn't get up. I sent the children to school and came home to keep all the picnic items that I had prepared the night before whilst he slept. But here's the thing with my Warrior, he wanted to make me happy. He woke up at almost mid-morning, got ready and said, "Dinda, go Google where we can go for brunch. Nice place, not the usual. It's our tenth anniversary."

I couldn't believe it. He tried! We drove to Penny University, 20 minutes from where we lived. We shared chicken and waffles, an affogato, and a Rocher cake. A quiet brunch in booth seats, that was our tenth anniversary, the last date we would ever have in a restaurant, the most special piece of memory. My Warrior tried and, true to his nature, did everything to make me happy.

After brunch, we stopped at a shop selling plants. He told me to pick a plant. Tenth anniversary, my realistic of a husband got me a plant instead of flowers. I picked one, and it is now growing steadily at our corridor.

We were only out for about two hours, and my Warrior spent the rest of the afternoon in bed, clearly exhausted. I appreciated his actions and told him exactly that. He smiled, kissed my forehead. "I love you. Happy Anniversary, Dinda."

Tenth and the last.

I got my last bouquet from my Warrior later in the month, a huge one with red roses and little fairy lights that lasted for days. He used to say flowers were all made for drama. But he bought them for me from time to time anyway because watching dramas was one of our favourite things to do together. And this bouquet was a surprise one, most extravagant.

"What's this for, Abang?" I was getting things ready for guests when the delivery came.

"For you because I love you and I appreciate you. You're a great wife." He smiled and kissed my forehead.

I wouldn't get any flowers from him anymore. I kept the little heart-shaped card.

TWENTY-ONE
June 2022

June was Father's Day month. I finally finished what I wanted to do since the prognosis, and it became my Father's Day gift for my Warrior and his entourage of five. I created a photobook for each of our five children filled with pictures of them with their Papa when he was not how he was now—"My Papa & Me" books. The healthy Papa who took us everywhere. I poured through pictures of birthdays, vacations, staycations, day-outs, carnival, car selfies, football training, first-times, births, bike rides, awards, and poses that were funny. When the photobooks were finally ready, I called them all to the living room. Together with their Papa, they looked through the photos individually, remembering what it was like and what happened behind each photo. We helped Naela and Nadra recall their photos as they were too young to remember.

My Warrior was so happy and was thanking me so many times. He went through each picture with each child, looking at all the experiences he had with them. He recalled them all, plus the funny stories behind them. That was to become memory books for the children. I cried so many times whilst sorting the pictures for the books. We will never have a repeat of those moments. Just like the moment their Papa looked through the books with each of them, that emotional moment would never be repeated.

My Warrior was looking through Arfan's when he stopped to tell Arfan, "No matter what, you're my family, my son." Not his stepson. He never treated Arfan as a stepson or any different from the rest. He felt for Arfan. He was worried for Arfan, and he loved Arfan. "Arfan is my son," he said.

Every time he had an argument with Arfan, he regretted. Every time Arfan was mad at him, he was sad. Every time Arfan came home late, he would be worried and asking me every five minutes.

"I only want Arfan to behave and not get bullied. I want Arfan to have respect. I want him to grow up happy and lead fulfilling life," he would say. "I scolded him because I love him." As any father would. And he had always hoped that Arfan knew that.

On the actual Father's Day, I got our Warrior a cake, also ordered pizza for the children, and we had a celebration. My friend sent over an ice cream cake. My Warrior was only up long enough for small spoonsful of cake. We've been having guests, and it exhausted him so much. Having guests meant that most of the time that he didn't, he'd be sleeping. It meant lesser time for his children to have chats with him. And this had paved the disengagement between the children and their Papa, something that my Warrior took as an opportunity to lessen his interaction with the children. When he passed, I seemed to notice this disengagement process. It was as if he was trying to make it happen so when the time came, the children would have lesser of a blow. His conversations with the children lessened over June. It was mostly only to me. Naela and Nadra would be misbehaving right next to him, and he would ignore them. Eshan could be watching TV with him, and he would just keep quiet. He never asked how Sarah's day was. He spoke to Arfan, but that was to help him sit up or to go get him something from the kitchen. I was pretty sure he must have said more to the children but not that I could see that month.

It was three weeks after his decline that he finally agreed for me to bring him outside, just around the neighbourhood. I got him all cleaned up, put him in his wheelchair, and got him out of the house, together with Sarah and Eshan, who were just waiting for time to zoom around in their skate scooters. They were also supportive of their Papa finally wanting to come out. It was just a short one of me pushing him in the wheelchair, enjoying some sun and wind. After about half an hour later, my Warrior wanted to go back home. He was getting tired. He thanked me and went for a nap.

June was also the school holidays. But because of my Warrior's condition, we couldn't take the children anywhere. We had to depend on friends and family to take them out. My Warrior was sad. "We always take them outside," he said.

That was when the hospice care's social worker asked him what he would like to do. He said he wanted to bring us all outside. He wanted the children to run around like we used to.

"Where would you like to go, Mr Selamat?"

"Marina Barrage. I always like it there."

My Warrior and I used to go for dates there. We also brought the kids for waterplay, kick the ball, and picnic. He also had flown his drone there late last year. That was one of his favourite places.

The hospice care linked us up with Ambulance Wish Singapore, an organisation that works on making the wishes of a terminally ill patient come true. The team contacted me and ironed out the details.

On 25 June 2022, the Ambulance Wish team arrived in the morning, ready to take us all out, the seven of us, plus my parents. My sister and her family of three were to meet us at the venue. My sister had also engaged a professional photographer to document the outing. We knew how precious this memory would be. I dressed the seven of us in matching hues, my sister had helped me get the children some new outfits for the day, and the family pictures looked amazing.

A lot of activities took place within the short hours outside. My Warrior was transported in a private ambulance, and I went along. My other family members had transport picking them up and sending them to the venue. Two ambulance attendants never left my Warrior's side, from the moment they picked him up at our home through all the activities at the barrage and sending him home. They made sure I never had to lift a finger to manoeuvre the stretcher. The Ambulance Wish Singapore team gave presents to the children based on their age and interest. They've set up a pizza lunch. They've got kites ready for my children to learn. They had a bouquet for me. They had a birthday cake for my father. They even had a book and a football signed by Fandi Ahmad, a local football legend.

My Warrior was in high spirits. He flew a kite whilst sitting on the stretcher. My mother flew it with him. He threw a football to Eshan, who was guarding the portable goal post that his Papa had bought for him. Eshan had a huge smile on his face and was very excited as well. We could tell how much he had missed his play time with his Papa. Football used to be the bond he had with his Papa. My Warrior wanted to train him so Eshan would play for his school team and be a national player.

He played bubbles with the twins. He drank juice. He cracked a smile throughout the time there, never complaining that he was tired. To watch him that day was absolute joy. He got what he wished for—to be outside. He was such an outdoorsy person; it was hard that he could no longer go out. He was a footballer, a boxer, a photographer, a sportsman, a lover of the outdoors. He had hopes that his children would also love being outdoors like he did. He soaked in the atmosphere. He watched the children. He smiled a lot.

The photographer took a lot of photographs, which turned out phenomenal. He captured moments that were so precious and truly for keeps. We were so grateful to everyone who made it extremely enjoyable and memorable. Even the weather cooperated with us. It was raining in the early morning, but soon the sun was out for us to just be outside and play.

He was extremely exhausted when we came home. But was in a joyous mood. He slept the entire afternoon very peacefully. I watched him sleep with an overwhelming sadness in my heart.

As soon as the photographer sent the softcopy of the pictures taken that day, I had them printed within the next few days. I wanted to have the album ready as quickly as possible so the children will freshly recall the day whilst still being excited. I wanted my Warrior to see the album and smile for that day again.

As my Warrior flipped through the album from his bed, he beamed and nodded. He saw what he had wished for, and the pictures spoke for the day itself.

"I love that day, and I love the pictures. Thank you for doing this so fast, Dinda." He smiled.

There was a little teddy bear that the Ambulance Wish team had given my Warrior. He held it in pictures. Naela asked her Papa if she could have the bear when we came home. Her Papa gladly gave it to her. And she has been sleeping with the bear since.

On 26 June 2022, Eshan started a new season for his football training. It began as a father-son thing from when Eshan was about four, a little bonding time for Eshan and his Papa. That day Eshan, now eight, headed for training without his Papa. He was picked up by a couple, arranged through his Papa's hospice care. As my Warrior was deteriorating, Eshan had missed a lot of training the last season. But he kept quiet, understood that it was impossible for his Papa to continue going with him. We asked the social worker at my Warrior's hospice care to help. They matched him with a couple who volunteered. Eshan could now continue the thing he enjoys. But I couldn't even imagine what was going through his head. He was very matured about it, never opposing the changes. My Warrior spoke to him before Eshan left for training that morning, advice a father would give his son, a sense of regret that he couldn't continue, but his hopes remained the same. He hugged his little boy. Eshan came home from training with detailed stories that he excitedly relayed to his Papa. His Papa smiled with pride and hugged him, sealed with a kiss on his forehead.

The new school term started, and we went on a routine. I would be up at 5:00 a.m., about the same time as Arfan would, and started with settling my Warrior in a sitting position. Then I'd get the children's breakfast ready, I'd prepare my Warrior's breakfast milk or juice as well. I'd then put away the dishes that was washed last night and wake the children up for school. I'd start showering Naela and Nadra once the three elder ones were at the breakfast table. I'd then have my shower whilst the children were all finishing up their breakfast, pray my *Subuh*, and get ready. Arfan would already leave for school by then. I'd then put my Warrior safely lying down in his hospital bed, and I'd leave Naela and Nadra at home with him whilst I send Sarah and Eshan to school. After 15 minutes, I'd be home to pick up Naela and Nadra to send them to their childcare centre. I'd be home 20 minutes later, get things prepared to shower my Warrior. This would take some time, and then I'd start with my work right next to him. In between, he'd ask for water, ice sticks, to chitchat, to watch a drama on TV that he was following, and I'd eat my breakfast or just have my coffee with him. At about 1:00 p.m., I'd go out to pick Sarah and Eshan up from school. This soon changed when Sarah and Eshan decided that they were ready to come home by themselves and relieved their Mommy of that midday duty. I'd have their lunch prepared whilst still working and look over their homework as well. Eshan would go for his Wednesday football training. I'd be working until 5:00 p.m. and then get dinner started before picking up Naela and Nadra from school. In between, I'd attend to my Warrior's needs and showered him at about 6:30 p.m. Except for Arfan, the other children keep to the 8:30 p.m. bedtime routine. They have to be in their beds by then. I'd be having my dinner next to my Warrior then and ended my chores with folding the clothes out the dryer. I'd usually chitchat with my Warrior whilst watching TV until he was sleepy. I'd then get the eye medication and place the tape and gauze on his right eye. This was done a few times a day. His right eye had developed ulcer by then and could no longer close. So some help was needed to make sure his eye was hydrated and protected. Once he slept, I'd tidy around the house and rest. He'd wake up every two hours, asking to sit. He'd clear his phlegm and then sat for a little while more before asking to lie down again. And that would be what it was throughout the night until I'm up again at 5:00 a.m.

On weekends, we'd have another set of routine; that included their religious classes, Sarah's tuition class, and Eshan's football Sunday.

We ran like clockwork.

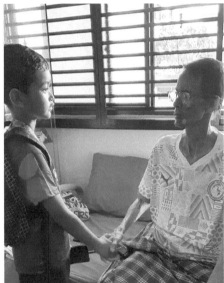

TWENTY-TWO

Faith and Fate July

My mother's birthday came. We had a little celebration at home with my cousin's family, who came for a visit. They came with eel soup. My Warrior loved eel. And he managed to eat a little of that soup. He also had a bit of cake. But his appetite was really low. I noticed he didn't even finish his protein shakes anymore. Half was the usual by then. He didn't ask for anything much but drinks and flavoured ice sticks and ice creams. I gave him whatever he asked for as long as he took something in.

Hari Raya Haji came. We had my parents over, my sister and her family, my best friend and her husband, my Warrior's sister's and his brother's families. The guys played darts, and my Warrior watched them. He had installed that dart board and bought a couple of dart sets when he could still walk. It was his joy. He had wanted friends and family who came by to play with him for a game or two. He did have that chance before his decline. I had helped him up from his bed and wheeled him near them so he could watch them play. He could only watch for a few minutes before asking to lie down again. By then, he had the tubes of the oxygen concentrator connected to his nose. We had asked for the hospice care to send it to us, along with the commode a few days earlier. My Warrior could no longer walk to the bathroom for his showers a few days back, and I've called for the commode so I could wheel him to the bathroom.

Weeks before, I was trained by the hospice care on how to properly care for my Warrior as he transitioned into fully bedridden. He was rapidly declining towards that stage; even talking had become difficult that he used a little white board to communicate. I wanted to be able to safely take care of him without causing more pain to his fragile body. I was already applying my newfound skill in transferring him safely from bed to chair, adjusting his position on the bed, properly showering him, even skincare for his diapering areas.

He was a neat and clean man who puts importance on hygiene and looking good. I, of course, wanted to continue that for him. I applied moisturiser on his arms and legs, serum on his face, and combed his hair neatly, always complimenting how handsome he looked once he's ready. His clothes would match, and bed would be clean and smelled nice. I had also shaved his face clean one day and clipped his nails. I wanted him to look the neatest, even though he could no longer look after himself. I was his other half; it was my duty.

I took a one-week leave from work because I wanted to concentrate on taking care of my Warrior. I just felt I needed to. And I loved that week because I really devoted my time to him. I did everything without rushing it. We talked, we joked, we laughed, we watched movies. My mind wasn't distracted with work and was focused on him. He appreciated it and stayed up a lot so he could keep me company, which made me laugh because I took leave to keep him company.

The day after Hari Raya Haji, 11 July 2022, I made him a glass of durian milkshake for brunch. I had blended pieces of durian that my brother-in-law brought the night before into his vanilla milk. He had managed to eat some small bites of the durian last night. He finished the whole glass! I was ecstatic. My parents had brought the children out to the beach that day, so we were home alone. And we had an ice stick date. I remembered him smiling a lot, even when he napped.

That night, after the children has gone to bed, I sat folding clothes just like I would. He was sitting by his bed. Suddenly, he started laughing, not the sickly laugh with voice so far away. It was a laugh that he had when he was healthy. It was a sound I've not heard in a long while. I looked at him and asked what was so funny and if he had a joke that he wasn't sharing.

He laughed again and said, "Semua dah okay. You okay. The children okay. The house okay. All is okay." And he laughed a bit more and smiled a long smile.

"What do you mean all is okay?" I asked.

He just continued smiling and nodded. "All okay."

I had asked if he wanted to shower that evening, and he said he just wanted me to wipe him clean. And I did just that, extra careful and strangely much slower, making sure I cleaned every area and didn't hurt him. I had even cleaned him up as he emptied his bowels. I was trained; hence, I was confident and thought nothing of it.

As usual, I looked at him in his clean clothes and smelling great, and I said, "Handsome dah, Abang. All done."

He smiled back at me and said, "Thank you, Dinda. You're perfect."

That night, he woke up two times to cough out his phlegm and to just sit at his bed. Nothing out of the ordinary, except he had a lot of phlegm that night, and he didn't ask for his painkillers. I kissed his cheeks when I put him back to bed.

Next morning, the usual routine started. I woke up and saw Arfan starting to sit my Warrior up. I told Arfan I'll take over and help my Warrior up. Before Arfan left for school, I saw him starting to put his Papa back to lying position, and again, I told Arfan that I'll take over and help him lie down. We all did our usual routine.

Only difference, at 7:40 a.m. on 12 July 2022, I came home from sending the twins to the childcare centre, and my Warrior had gone home to meet his Maker in his sleep. He was in the same position that I had left him.

My world stopped.

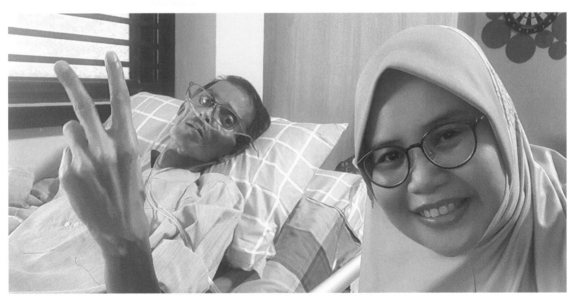

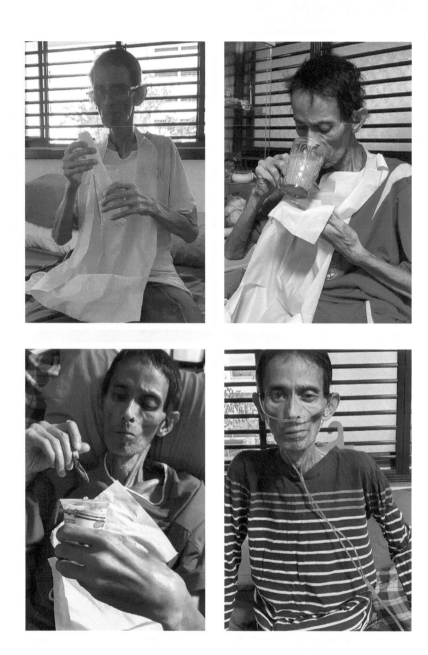

TWENTY-THREE

White

I promised that I'll accompany him on his final journey, and I promised we'll all wear white to match his final outfit. I fulfilled it. The children wore their Hari Raya outfit. His *kafan* was a piece of his own *kain ihram* from his Umrah. And I'm keeping the other piece.

He had wanted for the procedure to take place in the mosque as he didn't want his children to have any memory of his lifeless body being cleaned in our bathroom. He wanted it to be at Masjid Sultan, if it was possible, as that was where we were solemnised, where we got married, raring to start our new life hand in hand. But I was told that was not possible.

The journey from home to Masjid Maarof was terribly hard. I broke down a couple of times, heartbroken that he would not be coming home with me. The journey from Masjid Maarof to Pusara Abadi, the cemetery grounds, was strangely calming. He was all cleaned and miraculously looked nothing like his ill self. All the suffering seemed to have been lifted. Allah's will. He looked all serene to meet his Maker.

I was called in to customarily wash his face prior. I did it as gently as I did when he was alive. This was the face that lit up when I entered the room. It no longer did, and I will never see the face again. This was the face that sent butterflies to my stomach. It still did and forever will when I see his pictures or yearns for his presence. This was the face of a father who was so proud of his children. This was the face that I see first thing in the morning and last one at night for over ten years. This was the face I look for in a crowd. This was the face that made me felt so safe and so sure. This was the face that I fell in love with and will always love forever and a day, always.

On that day, as I left the burial plot, I knew that my life was no longer the same. I am now the grieving wife, the widow yearning for the wonderful soul who had left her. The grief will never leave as half of me had gone with him. As with the love that will never leave.

Good night, Kekanda. 'Til we meet again. I love you.

Al Fatihah.